CREATE FROM BEING

Guide to Conscious Creation

Table of Contents

Preface

Create from being,
Express by doing.

When that phrase first came to me in October of 2008, it made no sense to me. After a successful career in project management, and starting and operating my own businesses, I had a very strong mindset of making things happen by doing, by action. I had yet to learn that the greatest experiences of my life would be produced from "being" – which to me, at that time, was not an action verb.

We as humans are accustomed to the concept of creating by doing. Apparently we prefer to do things the hard way. There is only so much we can ever accomplish by doing. The creative process, which involves the Law of Attraction, is about creating from being. It is an easier, more natural, and more rewarding approach to life. Yet oddly enough, releasing the complexities of thought patterns to settle into the simplicity of it all can be a difficult undertaking, particularly for those of us who have taught ourselves that we can trust our thoughts more than our feelings as a guide to life. We EXPECT life to be complicated; we tend to distrust simplicity.

Only by timid experimentation here and there did I begin to truly realize for myself how this all works. This book is about what I have come to understand about life and the process of conscious creation, through my own experimentation.

The material in this book is gleaned from my observations and experimentations with my own life. I don't do much reading, and I don't readily adopt other people's ideas about life. I have always preferred to learn from self-experimentation, because then I KNOW what's real and how it works.

I was raised in a religious setting. By age twenty-five, that background no longer satisfied the questions in my curious mind. That was when I determined that I would no longer hold onto any belief simply because it was written in some book or was a tenet of some doctrine. I declared to myself that I would only believe that which I actually experienced, or that which made sense to me based upon my experiences.

My life has been marked here and there by experiences of what you might call a supernatural nature, since early childhood. Those experiences gave me a basis for realizing there is more to this existence than meets the eye. It was much more recently, about five years ago, that I began to find myself interacting and communicating at will with non-physical entities about how my life works.

You may choose to call it the voice of God, the Higher Self, Allah, angels, saints, the Universe, Jehovah, Buddha, Spirit, intuition, All That Is, or the small still voice within. Whatever your term of choice, there are different forms of spirit communication, and mine is clairaudience. That means that I hear audible voices and have very informative conversations with them. I choose to refer to them as my spirit guides, because they are not incarnate (spirits) and because they offer useful education and guidance for me along the way. They have different voices, unique personalities, different areas of interest, and endless patience (certainly a prerequisite for working with me!) They are very loving and attentive, never take vacations, and have encouraged me along the way when I have gotten discouraged. Time and time again their advice has proven to be effective within my life.

They have led me into a deeper understanding of Life and of my Self. They never make choices for me, but they always offer new perspectives to broaden my awareness of what is going on around me, and why. They never judge anything that I do, they simply educate me. Some of them have lived human lives on Earth, and others have not. They have guided and supported me along the path of experimentation that led to my understanding of the material within this book.

Wherever you encounter indented, italicized sections in this book, those are quotes from these conversations with my spirit guides. They occasionally use secular terminology (such as "God") and I have not changed that in the quotes.

Spirit communication is not a focus of this particular book, and my guides emphasize the importance of us making and understanding our own choices in life – which IS the point of this book. Very often spirit communication leads to a reliance on, or an expectation of, non-physical entities to make difficult life decisions for us – and this is the very reason that communication with them is not more common, frequent, or easily accessible. Guides never make decisions for us, they primarily educate and advise.

So this book is based upon my own observations and experiences of Life, with a bit of suggestion, guidance, and encouragement here and there from my spirit guides.

Throughout, I will use the terms "the Universe" and "All That Is". I prefer these terms to secular ones which have specific but different connotations for different groups of readers. That is simply intended to prevent readers from picturing what I say in the pre-defined cast of a particular personality, entity or connotation.

The terms "the Universe" and "All That Is" are not interchangeable. To me, "the Universe" refers to all consciousness that is presently external to my personal experience of being human as myself, and indicates all consciousness with which I interact to some level in the creative processes covered in this material. It actually is a co-creative process. My individuality, and hence my apparent differentiation from the rest of the Universe, is an illusion created for the human experience. I co-create with the Universe, and to me, you the reader are part of the Universe. I have created the experience of writing this book, and you have created the experience of reading it.

By contrast, "All That Is" refers to the unity of all consciousness that exists – including mine and yours. When I combine "me" with "the Universe" that adds up to "All That Is".

So feel free to replace these terms with your own as you read this book, if you do not find your terms to have predisposed definitions and limitations associated with them.

I would like to share with you a channeled message from the Earth about creation, and then we'll begin our discussion. Early one morning in 2008 as I sat watching the mist rise and swirl over a lake in southern California, a soft female voice began to talk to me, beginning the sequence of events which led me on my journey of writing this book:

I AM the creative energies of the earth – those which you mold into new experiences for you and for others.

Look into my mist; create from ESSENCE, not specifics. Tell us what YOU see. If you KNOW what you WANT, then the choosing becomes easy: others choose you and you choose them. Your FEELINGS know, sense, and create the future all at the same time.

It is merely up to you, and your mind, to CHOOSE. When all this is operating together, then ALL LIFE flows SMOOTHLY.

Life is a cluttered stage. Stay focused within the simplicity of your greatest, deepest, most passionate desires. Those who are ready to SHARE those with you will appear from the mist before your eyes. Think of it like a wishing well, you must KNOW what you want in order to attract it by its ESSENCE. See, feel yourself WITHIN an experience, and you will attract that which can provide THAT FEELING.

Make this a part of your awareness, and always keep your desires in the NOW. Those you plan for the future will never arrive because that is where you keep them – you always consider them to be in the future, and so they will never materialize in your NOW.

Each moment, understand exactly WHERE you are in re-lation to that which you desire.

Speak of your desires in the present. Love your desire, and in a new way. It is an essence, and you both attract and create it, simultaneously. Feel and know its essence. Want and feel the experiences you may have. Attract, draw them to you like a friendly pet eager to please, eager to play.

Your playful nature is your strongest vibration, because it is so accessible, it releases the conditionings of your soci-

ety and your adulthood, and it helps you to immediately access your emotions free of self-judgment. Combined with music, your playfulness is the center of your greatest creativity.

You underestimate the potential of your creativity and the life you may have. But we feel that you will learn along the way. It is our greatest joy to watch your unfoldment. Allow yourself to feel that!

I provide all that you need. Now I wish to provide you with ALL the EXPERIENCES you DESIRE.

Each moment, love and celebrate who you are, not what you do.

We love you dearly...

My Love to You,

Myke Wolf
San Diego, California
April, 2010

Introduction

You are creating your own life. Moment by moment, you continually create and attract all the experiences that fill each day, including those experiences which you enjoy, and those which you enjoy less. You attract each person, thing, opportunity and event into your experience. There is nothing in your life which you have not invited in some way.

In this present Now moment, you are creating your future, and attracting the future you created in very recent Now moments. Everything that is happening around you at this moment is a result of choices you have made in previous moments.

Every experience that you have throughout your life is created by, and attracted by, you. At some level, in some way, consciously or otherwise, you have asked for all that you perceive as being external to you.

Nothing is random. Nothing occurs without a specific purpose intended for one or more people. There are no mistakes. Planet Earth is the perfect stage and setting for humans to learn about the creative process, and that's why we come here lifetime after lifetime. Understanding and mastering the creative process is one of the most exciting journeys available here.

When you chose to come to Earth for this lifetime, when you were born, you inherited a very special birthright as a human being. Your birthright is that you, as a human being born onto Earth, are a co-creator, perfectly equal to all other human co-creators.

Every human on this planet is a co-creator who experiences the results of his or her conscious and sub-conscious choices. This includes all life experiences, events, things, and people we encounter.

And since you already are creating your own life, it stands to reason that understanding and becoming involved with that process would allow you to create a life filled with more joyful experiences.

The principles of this creative process are remarkably simple. They are consistent and straightforward. It is we humans who complicate things with overthinking, worries, and fears. It is we who often choose not what we really want, but what we think we deserve, and we thereby take paths in life which we deem to be less enjoyable.

The process of peeling back the layers of habits, beliefs, thoughts and behaviors which tend to create and attract less enjoyable experiences can run surprisingly deep, but is a worthwhile process, and certainly a necessary one if you seek a more enjoyable experience in life.

This book will guide you into a more complete conscious awareness of your role as the creator of your life. It is specifically designed to be read sequentially. The contents are deliberately ordered, and build upon each other as the book progresses.

Ultimately, however you choose to integrate these materials into your own life is a matter of your unique choice, and thereby ultimately enriches humanity as a whole. So I fully encourage you to take the pieces that you like and adapt them to your own understanding of your own life as you see fit. I certainly encourage you to experiment with the principles in your own life – that is why I have written this book.

And remember, you deserve to enjoy this journey through life – since you ARE creating it all!

Dedication

This book is dedicated to YOU. It takes great courage, dedication and honesty to venture outside the hustle-bustle of everyday mainstream life on a personal quest for deeper understandings about how Life works.

Life here is an individual journey, for while the Universal Laws operate the same for all of us without exception, we each have a unique identity, purpose and path to discover for ourselves. There are hints and clues along the way, but the journey to understanding Life is always an individually unique experience.

I offer you the material in this book from my own personal experience. Eighteen years ago I began the process of discarding everything I had been taught to believe, and began to accept only that which I personally experienced for myself. When you tell the Universe that you seek deeper understanding, be prepared for the reply!

Now I understand exactly why I know what I know, and that is a very secure feeling indeed. The more I learn, the more I realize I have yet to learn, but I have gained a solid foundation of understanding Life upon which to build as I continue along my own journey. The peace of mind I enjoy keeps me calm even when Life doesn't appear to go my way. If that is what you seek, then I truly hope you will find some of it here.

The "spiritual journey" held many surprises for me. I never expected that journey was an inward one – a journey to fully understanding the Self before getting too concerned about the external world, and to a more complete understanding of where that boundary really is. We do in fact create our own experience of the external world from within, from the Self, so that is a necessary starting point.

I also never expected that in order to love others unconditionally, I had to first learn to love myself – and it was an even greater surprise when I first realized that I didn't love myself unconditionally!

This journey necessitates a willingness to be absolutely honest with yourself, about yourself. There are many things we don't want to examine about ourselves, and those are usually the very things we must begin with and release in order to proceed.

So this book is written for you and to you, the spiritual seeker, wishing you joy as you experience the miracle of the life you are creating.

Dear Co-creator,

Life is the experiencing of Self.

At all times, remember who and where you are – a child of the Divine, in the perfect place and the perfect timing.

You are WITH your body, but you are NOT your body.

The birthright of Earth humans is the ability to create, and to be fully and completely supported within this endeavor. Even as you breathe, so do you create.

Never underestimate the potential within ANY moment to change your life – for it truly is limitless.

At all times, love who you are being, and enjoy what you are doing.

We see you, we know you, and we love you infinitely! For we are the Universe, and it is our greatest joy to co-create with you.

Foundation

We tend to identify ourselves by what we are doing: "I am an artist"; "I am a homemaker"; "I am a doctor"; "I am a student."

Yet the greater truth of who we really are is that each of us is an immortal, infinite, spiritual being, playing the role of a human. We are unlimited and unique within the Universe. We are at once part of All That Is, and simultaneously under the illusion of being a frail, mortal, error-prone, separate being as a member of humanity. There is a duality, a dichotomy, to the experience of being human.

For most of us, learning to look past our human aspects, to see who we are and whom we are being, is not an easy journey – at least it wasn't for me. It takes time and courageous exploration in order to separate who we are from who we think we are. It feels safe to cling to the person we have come to know ourselves to be throughout the course of our life, and a bit less safe to explore the deeper realities of our true identity. Knowing the difference requires the release of belief systems and thinking patterns we have accumulated throughout our lives.

Understanding who we are, and whom we are BEING, which are not the same, is certainly a first step in truly understanding and becoming aware of the process of conscious creation. Knowing where our consciousness is separate from our thoughts, beliefs and actions can be a difficult understanding to gain, but is quite necessary in order to remove those aspects that create and attract experiences which we don't enjoy into our lives. Becoming conscious of, and consciously involved with, the creative process we are already engaged in requires that we become more conscious of Self and of Life overall.

You have a relationship with your self, and you have a relationship with your life. You interact with each in a certain way which is driven by deeply embedded belief systems and thought patterns. These relationships are very influential in determining your expectations of Life, of what is or is not possible. Changing them can and will change your life. Knowing what you believe about your self and your life is necessary in order to identify what you would like to change. Changing your life begins with changing these relationships.

Before proceeding, it would be helpful to consider your own starting point. You already hold fundamental beliefs about Life, so start by yourself asking a few basic questions in order to determine what you really do believe:

- Do you believe that you are here on Earth, with intentional purpose, or do you believe that you are a byproduct of a random cosmic anomaly?
- Do you see the Universe as supportive of your life and experience, or do you see the Universe as adversarial to you?
- Do you have a fundamental belief that you are able to attain a more enjoyable and fulfilling life for yourself, or do you feel your life is subject to the whims of unseen forces over which you have no control?
- Are you defined by what you enjoy, and by following your own desires, or do you adapt to what you believe your environment and those around you demand or expect of you?
- Are you enjoying your life completely, or do you wish for change?
- Do you believe that you deserve any changes that you may wish for within your life?

Take some time with these questions. Write your answers down and read them to yourself. Which answers feel good to you, and which do not?

These answers are your own personal starting point to the material within this book. Know and acknowledge where you are in relation to your beliefs about what is or is not possible within your own life. Be very honest with yourself. Those very beliefs drive what you have been experiencing lately in your life.

This book is not about magic, it is about the mechanics of the creation process. That process of creation will not change you, it is up to you to know and change your beliefs in order to create and attract different experiences into your life. That IS what this book is all about – discovering, knowing, and exploring these beliefs.

This first section, Foundation, will assist in bringing a greater realization of these aspects to the surface, to the level of conscious awareness, which will form the structure for stepping into the full discussion of how we create within our lives, and how we can change what we experience.

Being Human

Welcome to Earth, you're a human being. (You probably already knew that.)

That means many things, and one of them is that you are inherently "human". When we say that, we automatically know what is meant – that we do things we perceive to be mistakes, and that we (sometimes) learn from them.

Let's start by eliminating that word from our vocabularies – mistakes. After all, don't they produce opportunities for learning? We don't know something won't work until we try.

What if we repeat the same action several times, and keep getting the same result, and chide ourselves for being "stupid" enough to repeat it? We like to say, "I knew better than to make that mistake again!" Maybe so, but in repeating the action and getting the same result, perhaps what we were learning was to slow down and think before acting in the first place. There is always learning involved in anything we consider to be "mistakes" – even ones that we repeat, and even if the learning is not so obvious.

You are human – so accept it, and learn to laugh at yourself a bit. Easy to say, but harder to do, isn't it? I have always been unnecessarily hard on myself. Looking back, I can see that earlier in life I truly had an expectation that I should be perfect, and that every mistake I made indicated some area I needed improve about myself. It never occurred to me that I didn't expect anyone else to be perfect – just me. I was trying to prove something to myself, and that was completely unnecessary.

One day I started looking at myself as if I were an actor in a TV sitcom. When I would make a "mistake", I would step outside myself and look at the situation from the perspective of a TV viewer watching a scripted, intentional folly. Much to my surprise, I began laughing – because I knew how funny I would consider the situation if watching someone else do it. That technique helped me to instantly relax my attitude about the situation, and over time I began to relax my overly ambitious and self-defeating self-expectations. I learned to laugh at myself in place of criticizing myself.

Understanding and interacting with the creation process requires experimentation, leading to what we usually call trial-and-error. In truth, there is no "error", because we always create and experience exactly what we meant to – the only error is in our own misunderstanding of how and why we DID create it.

What if one purpose of being here is to explore or learn about the creative process? Then all outcomes from experimentation, or trial, become successes, not errors.

If we become attached to a specific outcome in any situation, instead of simply exploring the joy in comparing what we thought we wanted to what we actually created and experienced, then we are robbing ourselves of the true and continual joy available to us here on Earth as human.

If we understood EXACTLY how to work the creative process to get EXACTLY what we expected, then we wouldn't be here anymore – it would simply be too boring. The attraction of life here is that it seems unpredictable.

In order to get the full benefit of the material in this book, I suggest opening yourself up to experimentation with these principles for the purpose of learning, without judging the outcomes to be mistakes. Accept yourself as human, be kind to yourself, and be willing to laugh at yourself.

Accepting Change

Change is a fact of life, it is a certainty. Life will not remain the same, and if we expect it to, then we cause ourselves unnecessary difficulties and worries. Life feels much smoother when we learn to embrace change and see the potentials of the new opportunities being presented.

Allowing ourselves to embrace change, instead of fearing it, leads to a more enjoyable life. It is helpful to realize that we create all change that we experience in life, and that we create this change in order to continue growing and learning.

Change means that something in life has served its purpose and that we have outgrown it. That is cause for celebration, not worry. Instead of wondering what we did wrong, we could consider what we did right.

Now, that can be easier to say than to actually do. The sudden loss of a job, which I have certainly experienced, can feel unexpected and can provoke thoughts of fear, worry, lack, and "what did I do wrong?" Yet every life change I have experienced, when seen in retrospect, ultimately led to situations which I enjoyed far more. I am not downplaying the apparent difficulties that can accompany transition from one job to the next, but I am saying that we do have a tendency to perceive those transitions as being harder than they really are. We tend to hold onto the past as if the future could not be better. We like to feel safe, and not knowing the future can feel unsafe at times.

Psychologists generally agree that changes such as job loss, the ending of relationships or marriages, and moving to new homes create high degrees of stress in our lives. I disagree. I suggest that the RESISTANCE we build, the fear of change, is what creates that stress. Happily, it is completely within your own power to dramatically reduce that stress factor by accepting change instead of resisting it.

One approach, which I have slowly begun to adopt over the years, is to view change with excitement and anticipation. I have learned to reflect upon similar changes in the past, and see what I eventually did gain – a job I was happier with, a relationship that was better suited for me, or a home that felt more comfortable and harmonious. Then I become honest with myself about the aspects of the ended situation I had been overlooking, ignoring or simply putting up with – perhaps an unkind boss, an unsupportive partner, or a home that didn't feel right in some way. I have come to view change as something that simply brings the next adventure into my life, and have begun to see it as an opportunity to attract a better situation.

When some major aspect of life changes dramatically, more often than not it is because we have outgrown the situation and to stay longer would stymie our continuing personal spiritual growth. We created and attracted that job, home, or relationship into our lives for a reason, and we have now grown beyond it. Our vibration has changed, and just as we created the situation in the first place, we now magnetically repel it from our lives because it no longer serves us.

My guides like to remind me at such times that I should be celebrating. I like to remind THEM that they don't have bills to pay, and that they have never helped me to pack a box or move a chair! I know they are right, but it can be tough sometimes to see beyond the present circumstances and find a silver lining to what appears to be a huge, dark thundercloud.

As you explore the creative process within your own life, you may find yourself experiencing more, not less, change. I certainly did, and at first it was unsettling. I was seeking the feeling of stability from my environment, and life tossed me around until I learned that stability and security come from within. When I began to feel solid and peaceful within myself, significant changes in my "outside" life no longer scared me, and life presented a more secure feeling environment for me. Your experience may be very different, but when you pursue a path of spiritual growth and realization, your life WILL change to reflect the new you. Fortunately, the changes attracted by spiritual growth do lead to a more joyful life, and life does become gentler.

Perfection Redefined

Perfection is often defined as a standard, a state of having no flaws or imperfections. The shortcoming with that definition is that flaws are defined subjectively. Some define perfection as being "complete". I posit that both definitions contradict the very experience of being human, from the standpoint of pure definition.

How would you define perfection for humanity? A person that never makes mistakes? Just using the word mistake places a judgment on an experience. Part of being human is to explore the ability to choose different experiences.

There never has been, and never will be, a perfect human, even if it were objectively definable. That is who we already are at a soul level, and we come here for a different kind of experience.

I see perfection as more of a process than an end-goal. Enigmatic and esoteric as usual, this is how my guides define perfection:

Perfect for you is that which perfects you.

A popular, and excellent, analogy is the diamond-in-the-ruff, which looks like a dark rock until it is cut, abrased and polished into a cut, finished, glittering gemstone. It is often the difficult times in life which help us to see the beauty already hidden within.

The thinking that perfection is a standard to be achieved places undue and stressful expectations upon ourselves. It also sets an ambiguous, subjective goal which requires us to exercise self-judgment in order to monitor progress; a goal which, I feel, is contradictory to the experience of being human in the first place.

One of the healthiest things that I ever learned to do was laugh at myself instead of judging myself when I felt I had made a mistake or done something in error.

When we are not so focused on achieving a standard which doesn't exist, then it becomes much easier to relax and focus on the experience of being here, the experience of being human.

In a sense, our soul already is complete or perfect. That's why we come to Earth for the human experience – because we can't have this experience in our soul state. Did you ever think of it that way? Did you ever consider that maybe we come here to actually experience the difficult times as well as the fun times, the bike tumbles that lead to a scraped knee, the chill of a cold night, or the uncertainty life seems to excel in providing? Did you ever wonder if the soul, understanding its immortality and wisdom, would seek an experience where it would sometimes have the illusion of feeling unsafe, unloved, or vulnerable?

I remember an epiphany moment that occurred a few years ago. Several people had expressed concern to me about all the gloom, doom and injustice in the world. I had a sudden realization – what if Earth already IS perfect, for the purpose that she serves? What if the purpose of Earth is to provide the experience of the illusion of danger and uncertainty and fear? What if courage in the face of such emotions is one of the experiences we come here for? That experience would certainly not be possible in our soul state, because in that state we always know that we are immortal and safe.

Choosing to view every moment and every experience as perfect for us is certainly constructive for the creative process, when we consider that we have created each of those experiences. It can help to release thoughts of worry or fear so that we can see the deeper purpose and meaning in those experiences, and learn more about ourselves and the creative process from them.

When to Forgive Yourself

We humans certainly can be pack rats when it comes to emotional baggage. We carry stuff from the distant past along with us, bogging us down unnecessarily. Remorse, regrets, and ruminations are not conducive to the creative process, because they bring an un-enjoyed past forward into the Now moment, from which we are creating our future.

The moment a situation has occurred, it is in the past – it is over and done. Once a situation is in the past, its only value to the present Now moment in which we are creating our own future is in whatever we learned from the experience of the situation.

We tend to label ourselves from past events. We may call ourselves insensitive for not anticipating that a certain joke or comment would be taken personally by someone we care about; we may call ourselves clumsy for accidentally breaking a dish; we may call ourselves careless for locking the keys in our car and missing a meeting we consider to be important.

Over time, these perceptions of ourselves accumulate. We sometimes develop a sense that we are undeserving and unworthy, and we emotionally feel this. Each time we recall these scenarios, as we tend to do often, we confirm the emotion and with it our conclusion that we are careless, clumsy, insensitive, or a host of other pet adjectives.

This behavior is not helpful in the processes of creating and attracting enjoyable experiences for ourselves, because we won't attract what we don't feel worthy to receive, even if we have already created them.

Fortunately we have a process called "letting go" that is as easy as it sounds. We are choosing to recall those events and relive those emotions, and it is just as simple to recall them differently and choose a more uplifting emotion for the experience. We are choosing to recall the experience, so we can just as easily change the remembering of it, and the way we feel about it while remembering it.

Although I titled this topic "self-forgiveness", there are times when the phrase "letting go" is more appropriate. Forgiveness implies that a wrong has been intentionally and willfully committed. Forgiving oneself for prior actions which are now regretted is a choice, a decision, that can be easily made. However, it is not necessary in the process of letting go to blame ourselves for the action. To me, the very word "forgiveness" implies blame, and even if we "forgive" it, we are still considering that past experience to have been our "fault". Letting go is different – it is a more complete release, without the self-judgment.

In cases of negligence, accidents, or carelessness, I prefer to use the phrase "letting go". I don't see the point in forgiving myself for simply being human. Accidents are called accidents for a reason – we did not willfully intend for them to occur. Forgiveness implies that we blame ourselves for a situation. While it may be appropriate to take responsibility for the outcome, such as replacing or repairing something we accidentally broke, that is different from blaming ourselves that it happened in the first place.

When past events come to mind that don't feel good to you, consider why they doesn't feel good. You can choose to see past situations differently, which will alter how you feel about them when the memories pop up again in the future. And that can have powerful effects on the creative process and on your future, in many different ways.

I have experienced allergies to cats most of my life. During a stay with a friend that had cats, I was taking allergy pills daily. In a conversation it came up that as a young boy I felt it unfair that I never was allowed to have a puppy, but my sister had a cat. I decided to replay those memories in my head, giving myself a puppy, and seeing my sister and I both playing with the cat and the puppy together, as a happy memory. The cat allergies vanished that day. To me, this was a tangible example of how we can view our past differently to effect a change in our now. It also was a demonstration to me of the power of the past, or our resistance or reaction to the past, in our minds.

If self-forgiveness doesn't apply, and letting go doesn't seem to work for you, then sometimes finding the humor in a situation can help. We tend to take ourselves very seriously. Often if we were to watch one of our own scenarios on a TV comedy show, with actors playing our role in the situation, we would find them funny, and would laugh at ourselves. I have found this technique to be helpful in letting go of self-judging emotion attached to past events.

We are all human, and we are all here learning from our own experiences. That is a fundamental part of being here, and there is no need to hold those very same experiences against ourselves, particularly when they interfere with the process of creating and attracting more joyful experiences into our lives. We aren't here to become "perfect", we are here to experience being human.

Abundance of What?

What does abundance mean to you? The recent western popularization of the topic of abundance has produced a proliferation of imagery including estate-like homes, fast cars, fabulous parties, private jet airplanes, chauf-ferred limousines, butlers, and overflowing bank accounts.

So, what is abundance?

> *Abundance is having more than enough of that which sat-isfies your deepest desires.*

Do tangible possessions such as cars, homes and money satisfy our deepest desires? Maybe. Or, perhaps some of our deepest desires are about how we want our life experiences to feel to us, but it's easier to picture that in a setting using these tangible things as the backdrop.

We do have a tendency to think of abundance in material terms. When we find ourselves wanting a hot sporty convertible, is it really about the car itself? Or, does picturing ourselves driving that car appeal to a deeper desire? Is it possible that the car represents something else – perhaps freedom, or prestige, or youth, or some other feeling we wish to experience more of?

Identifying what it is that we actually desire, not just the icon that repre-sents it, is very helpful in connecting with those opportunities that offer that experience, even if it's not in the form of that sporty convertible. And that would also help us to recognize such opportunities as they arise.

Life always IS abundant – with opportunities. Life DOES offer us opportu-nities for what we express that we most want. However, Life is not usually listening to our thoughts about a sporty convertible, but rather to our heart expressing a desire for more freedom in life. There is no shortage of opportunities, but there is sometimes a lack of recognition of the opportuni-ties when they appear, if they don't fit a preconceived expectation or image. That feeling for more freedom in life, represented by wanting that sporty convertible, could just as easily manifest in our lives in the form of a sudden and unexpected ending to a restrictive marriage or relationship, for example, or a new job that allows a more flexible schedule. We always do create and attract opportunities for experiences that will provide the essence, the feeling, of our deepest desires – even if we don't always recognize it at the time.

Life abundantly gives us what we express that we want, through our strongest and deepest desires. However, it will also reinforce what we believe we deserve, and that can prevent us from connecting with opportunities that we have created for ourselves. We'll discuss that in a later section.

There is also a twist to the topic of abundance. If we focus on wanting or needing more money, and put more emphasis on that than on enjoying what we already have, or if we perceive more money to be a need, then Life will abundantly deliver exactly what we focused upon – the lack of money, not the having of and enjoying of the experiences that more money can provide.

As you explore the creative process, it would be useful to recognize that Life interacts with you, providing you with an abundance of what you feel most deeply. Abundance is not something that you need to seek, chase, or create – you already ARE creating abundance in your life. *You continually create an abundance of opportunities for experiences that are likely to result in you feeling the way you want to feel.* If you are finding an abundance of experiences in your life which you are not enjoying, then you can create an abundance of a different kind within your life.

Seeing the abundance that you already ARE creating in your life, and understanding how you have created it, will help you to change the kind of opportunities that you create for yourself in the future. That will be a progressive theme throughout this book.

A New Way to Measure Success

Different people measure "success" in very different ways. One person may consider himself successful by financial standards. Another person may consider herself successful for creating a healthy family and a happy home. It certainly is an individualized ideal. Whatever the standard, it is related to our individual expectations for our lives. And if we don't attain that which we define as success within our lives, then we assume that we have somehow failed – and that is never true.

So let's try re-defining success to be "having an experience". Everything that we do in life IS an experience, so that makes us all very successful indeed. Isn't that a nice feeling? It certainly takes the pressure off, doesn't it? I find that it also makes it much easier to enjoy the journey and take time to smell the flowers along the way.

My definition of success really is not so far-fetched. If we are here to learn and understand ourselves and the creative process through experimentation, then every experience we have IS a learning experience, which does make every experience a success. And within that definition, we succeed at everything that we experience, merely by having experienced it.

Say that you decide to take up painting. What would you do? You would probably go buy easels, brushes, paint, and all the other supplies and tools you might need. You may buy a few books, or perhaps enroll in some art classes. And you would certainly experiment with different styles of painting, and different subjects. But perhaps in the end you aren't satisfied with the results. Perhaps people don't buy your art pieces; or maybe you find that you don't enjoy painting as much as you thought you would.

Did you fail or succeed? Did you fail as a painter? Or, did you succeed in learning that painting is not your forte? That depends upon your definition of success – your expectation of the outcome.

You did succeed in creating the experience of painting. You wanted to experience being a painter, and you did. Did you have a further expectation of an outcome that wasn't realized? Did you see yourself becoming a world-renowned artist selling pieces for large prices? If so, then perhaps you were more interested in fame or income through the means of painting, rather than simply having the experience of being a painter. Much of our definition of success is connected with our predefined expectation of an outcome.

If we choose to bog ourselves down with calling an experience a "failure" simply because its outcome didn't match our expectations, then we are judging the entire experience based upon one aspect. Instead, we could celebrate that we had a new experience, one that we created, and that we learned something about ourselves in the process.

In the creative process, it's not productive or helpful to limit an experience by creating a set of expectations for its outcome, and it certainly isn't helpful to judge an experience as "bad". Since we create all experiences in our lives, with purpose, it's not constructive to call our own creations (our experiences) "bad".

When I completed my personal bankruptcy a few years ago, my guides congratulated me on my success. I didn't particularly appreciate that comment at the moment, as I was very much engulfed in a sense of having failed miserably at something. They explained that my heart had been longing for freedom and peace of mind in life, and so Life abundantly offered a situation where bankruptcy became the only recourse. I had succeeded in creating exactly what my heart most wanted. My self-judgment in calling the experience a personal failure on my part was perfectly inaccurate from their perspective. My life did become more peaceful and less stressful without all the bills, so I did succeed in creating what I really wanted.

If you can begin to celebrate all experiences in your life as successes, by evaluating them for what you learned from them, or by learning to understand how you created the experience, or by the mere fact that you created them in the first place, it will change the energy in your life rather immediately and dramatically, and you will begin to create more enjoyable experiences for yourself. You will also begin to enjoy the added benefit of enjoying life as an experience, not as a competition against yourself.

The Purpose of Relationships

Other people are undeniable participants in our own creative process. It is very accurate to call us all "co-creators", because while we create for our own experiences, we seldom create experiences that do not in some way involve other people. A built-in aspect of the creation process is that we do attract others interested in sharing particular experiences with us.

We love to take pride in our accomplishments – the things we build, the acts we do. But to me it seems that our relationships along the way, our connections and interactions with others, are what really matters – the rest is just the backdrop or setting to play out those interactions.

We form a relationship with each person we encounter, no matter how brief. In any exchange there is a relationship, a way in which we relate to each other. If you think back over your life, you may be surprised to recall that sometimes brief, chance encounters with strangers that you never saw again left more of an impression on your life than long-time friends or relatives.

In each encounter with each person, we have the opportunity to present an uplifting experience, or the opposite. Cashiers, waiters, co-workers, friends, family members, boyfriends, wives, children – these are all examples of relationships serving very different purposes.

Many years ago I came to the conclusion that our interactions with others is how we experience our lives here. At age twenty-five, I decided to set aside all that I had been taught to believe, by religion or otherwise, in order to experience the Universe myself and choose the beliefs that fit that experience. It became very important to me to have a set of beliefs that matched and explained my actual experience in life. I began to look around me, and form some initial conclusions as I evaluated my own view of the Universe based upon my own impressions.

I once read that a human body contains some 75 trillion cells. I thought of atoms, which make molecules, which form amino acids and other building blocks to life, which subsequently combine into constructs such as DNA, finally making those cells. The cells themselves organize into tissue groups, which form organs, of which our bodies have many. Plants, animals, minerals, gems, rocks – all spanning an amazing range of variety. The atmosphere, with just the right mix to sustain the grand variety of life hosted upon this planet for untold eons of time, somehow maintained long enough to allow the continuity of life this planet has enjoyed. All the while Earth being only one of several planets accompanied by untold millions of comets, asteroids, and moons, all orbiting the Sun, which is only one of about a hundred billion stars in our galaxy, with another hundred billion or so other galaxies reaching as far as our strongest telescopes can peer. If each of those stars hosts about 10 planets like ours, then the number of total planets (not even including moons, asteroids, and comets) is a one with 23 zeroes after it.

My first conclusion, as I considered the intricate delicacy, balance, complexity, extent, and beauty of all that I could see – from the microscopic to the cosmic – was that there was a Design. Despite all the theories I had been taught in science class about how biological life just "happens" like some cosmic accident, there was simply too much going on for me to accept the thought that all this had just "happened" somehow by mere chance and luck.

My second conclusion came immediately and seemed quite obvious to me – if there is a Design, then doesn't it stand to reason that there is a Designer? Doesn't everything come from somewhere and something? There must be an origin for the Design, and in simplistic terms it seems that there must be some form of consciousness, or awareness, in order to have made a decision at some point to create, and what that creation would be like.

My third conclusion wasn't far behind. Given the complexity, the scale, the intricacy of all that I could see, the Design was not a small effort, not a simple task. Would any Designer go to all the trouble to create all this without some kind of purpose, some sort of reason? It seemed only logical that there must be a reason or purpose behind such an elaborate design.

What could that reason be? What could be the value, the purpose, in being here, as a human? After such great progress beginning to build my own personal belief system, one that actually made good sense to me in just a single day, I was stumped. The question faded away, and years began to slip by I busied myself with life and career.

Thirteen years later, on a business trip, I found myself sitting in the Dallas-Fort Worth airport waiting for a flight connection. Somehow, for some reason, that question drifted back into my head. I was exhausted – my job involved frequent travel, I was always busy and always on the go, and sometimes it seemed like I spent more time traveling than working.

I absently looked around the busy airport terminal, and found myself watching people. I began to observe their interactions with each other, and although I could not hear the conversations across the noisy terminal, I began to notice for the first time how easy it was to feel the tone of an exchange. Simply watching expressions, hand gestures, and body language, I could easily tell the kind of conversation others were having, and what emotions they were feeling. I watched a couple arguing. The woman seemed fine until the man began to become obviously agitated towards her. I could see her slump and cower, and her face took on a dejected expression.

Relationships ... interactions. As a human here, perhaps the most significant part of our experience, both in terms of time and importance, is our interaction with other people. But why? What is the purpose of these interactions?

Relationships and interactions with others are important in the way that we learn about ourselves through them.

One saying that has stuck with me for years states that relationships are for a reason, a season, or a lifetime. I believe ALL relationships are for a reason, it's just that some "reasons" take longer than others. There is no relationship in our lives that doesn't serve a purpose. The reason just isn't always immediately obvious – or perhaps we don't always take the time to realize it.

I have learned that life is about learning to see who we are being through our interactions with others, and we attract people into our lives at the right time to see those aspects which that person is perfectly suited to reflect back to us. It always works two ways – there is always something that person can discover from the interaction as well.

Earlier in life I was very focused on what I was doing, to the extent that I didn't pay that much attention to the people that came in and out of my life.

Lately I have learned that types of situations with people will repeat until I realize that it's about me – people are in my life to reflect back something about myself, like a mirror, that I want to see. Once I "get it", my life situations – and often some of the relationships in my life – change or end.

Somehow we tend to expect all relationships to continue on, and are repeatedly shocked when they end. But we all experience personal growth at different rates and in different directions, and often we simply grow apart. I have noticed within my own life that during times of rapid spiritual or inner growth, new people enter my life more often, and old relationships fall away more frequently.

When relationships do end, sometimes the circumstances are uncomfortable, and we part through disagreement. My guides always suggest, "bless and release". When friendships or partnerships end, there are sometimes hurt feelings or resentment. It's not helpful for your vibration to carry either forward with you as emotional baggage, because of what that would attract into your life.

"Bless and release", to me, means wishing the person well, and not choosing to carry resentments forward. Choosing to remember events that don't feel good to us is exactly that – a choice – and we can simply stop choosing to do that. I'm not suggesting that you deny your emotions, which do need to be expressed, but I am suggesting to move on quickly – change your focus to something more uplifting. Dwelling on anger, hurt or resentments from the past will only serve to attract more of the same into our immediate future.

Releasing does require honesty with Self! Saying that we have let something go, while still brewing about it inside, does not work! Be in touch with your feelings, in honesty, when releasing. Be genuine about wishing the best for the person that has left your life. Be grateful for what you have learned from them – because you are the one that requested, through your vibration, that they enter your life in the first place.

When people leave my life, I make the choice to recall the "good times" and the better side of the person. Regardless of the circumstances, it doesn't feel good to me to carry resentments. There is always a gift – something to be learned about ourselves through our interactions with others.

As you proceed with experimentation in the creative process, pay special attention to the timing and reason that people enter your life. Acknowledge that you and that person have co-created the relationship for a reason, and ask yourself why. Remind yourself that nothing is random. And maintain a good and respectful attitude towards all the people in your life.

Going Within

I don't meditate. At least, not in the traditional sense.

Now, that's not to say that I don't believe in meditation, in fact quite the opposite. Many people I know center themselves and gain personal benefit from meditative practices. For me, sitting in a certain pose, closing my eyes, and telling my mind to be quiet creates the exact opposite effect – a chattering mind. I like to be active, so my mind rebels. I do realize I could devote the time and train the mind with some form of meditation routine. But I like being active, and instead have learned that my "meditation" is more easily and naturally achieved in other ways.

What is the purpose of meditation? The common thread among most forms of meditation is to quiet the mind in order to receive – to receive messages, to hear that little voice within, to erase all the noise of the external world long enough to connect with the inner world. In this, meditation is certainly a worthwhile pursuit, particularly in today's frenetic societal pace.

Becoming more conscious of the creative process, and the messages that Life offers, is well supported by setting time aside for introspection, centering, and reflection. We quickly forget how much takes place within the span of a single day, and taking opportunities a few times a day to review is helpful in achieving a deeper understanding of what is really happening in our lives.

If you don't already have a form of meditation in use, try one. There are various types of group and individual meditation, as well as yoga, and various forms of exercise.

Since traditional meditation styles don't work for me, I have learned to hear my own inner voice, as well as those of my helpful spirit guides, in other ways. Something that works well for me is hiking. When I am away from my desk and immersed in nature, I am not thinking about my to-do list, schedules, appointments, or phone calls. I am able to enjoy the fresh air and beautiful surroundings, and my mind automatically relaxes. Then it is easy to converse with my guides.

As I began to develop my channeling I found that nature was my best meditation. Sitting under a tree, or walking through a beautiful park, or lulled into a relaxed state by the rhythm of the ocean waves, soothes my mind. I meditate in this way with my eyes and ears open, drinking in the sounds of chattering birds, the wind rustling through leaves, sunlight dancing over the crests of playful waves, the sun warming my face, breezes caressing my hair, the fragrance of nearby flowers. Nature quiets my mind, and then I can hear those quiet, patient, loving voices.

My channeling, my clairaudience, actually began in the shower – which, I quickly discovered, is not conducive to having pen and paper handy to write important realizations as they stream in!

Why the shower? I am not at my computer, I am not on the phone, I am not in a meeting. It's just me, and it's a purely physical experience, so my mind figures there's nothing for it to do, and it takes a little break. I am not worried about the day's schedule, I am not pondering incidents from the day before, I am just – showering.

Another tool that helps me to maintain conscious awareness as I continue my own exploration and learning of the creative process is journaling. I have now been journaling continuously for five years, and that has gotten me through the most exhilarating and the most challenging moments of my adult life.

I begin each day with it, and end each day with it. This helps me to keep my focus on the desires and dreams I am creating, and the exciting synchronicities that happen along the way. At times when a little inspiration is useful, I have plenty of reminders that life is not just about the ordinary daily routine which can sometimes be easy to slip back into.

The importance of listening within is to balance out the messages that Life on the outside seems to be giving. When we create from being, our being is within us, as we are about to discuss. The more often we can tune into that inner state, the more firmly rooted we remain on our own path of personal creation. The outer world is the result of the inner world.

Whatever your method of choice, centering within is extremely useful on the spiritual journey, for the sake of integrating all the experiences we have on a daily basis, connecting the synchronicities, and keeping our desires and dreams alive.

In a meditative state we can connect with inner peace and self-reflective thoughts that are easily drowned out by the din and pace of our daily activities. Whatever time of day works for you, whatever method works best for you, as you proceed with applying the material in this book it is helpful to set some time aside for that introspection and reflection. As you explore the creative process in your own life, you may find that meditative periods will help you to connect dots and begin to see the patterns in your day's events that you may have otherwise missed.

With a bit of foundation laid, we are ready to begin discussing how it is that we create from being, and what "being" really means.

CREATION

The topics we have covered up to this point were for increasing your conscious awareness of areas of your life that are important to the creative process, which we are now ready to discuss. There are three steps to the creative process:

- Create
- Attract
- Receive

Each step is equally important in order for us to experience what we have created for ourselves. Once we have created an experience we must attract it into our lives, in order to be able to recognize and receive it. Receiving it often includes the choice of whether or not we will actually take the opportunity for that experience when it materializes. How we actually perceive and enjoy the experience shapes and refines what kinds of opportunities we create next.

Let's begin by being very clear about "what" we create:

> We create opportunities for experiences that may include people, things, and events – experiences designed to provide a specific feeling

We create opportunities for experiences with a goal in mind – to provide us with a specific feeling. We tend to look at opportunities based upon how we expect them to turn out, not how we expect them to help us FEEL. We'll go into that differentiation more deeply later in this section.

Creating is the most automatic part of the creative process. We are doing it all the time. It's what we do, we are co-creators. I tend to focus in this material on the individual role, as we can only create for ourselves. Yet we as humans are closely connected to many other people at any given point in our lives – far more than we tend to consciously realize – and most of our creative activity interacts with one or more of them, intended to produce experiences involving more than just one person.

My early concept of creation, from my religious upbringing, was that everything we see, even those things visible only through telescopes and electron microscopes, was created in six days: wheels were set in motion, the planet was populated, life as we know it began. Creation was a one-week event, done at the beginning of time, all handled, wrapped up and finished, nothing for us to concern ourselves with. This was all due to a singular God entity, which handled all the aspects of creation so that we could simply show up and enjoy it.

This concept was so deeply engrained in me that, despite my intention to unlearn doctrines in order to open myself up to greater truths about the Universe, I resisted the conversation when my guides began to discuss my role as the creator of my own life.

However, ignoring them did not prevent me from creating within my own life, for the truth of the matter is that we do indeed create and attract ALL that we experience in life. I continued to create, while thinking I was merely a victim of some process I didn't fully understand, perhaps something I deserved, or maybe something I needed to learn – I grandly created a glorious financial bankruptcy in my life, a really spectacularly un-enjoyable one, despite having a successful business.

I am not saying that ignoring your inner voice will lead you into financial hardship. But I am saying that all experiences we encounter in life are the result of our desires, beliefs, choices, thoughts, and subsequently, our actions. It is up to us to direct whether we are creating enjoyable experiences or less-than-enjoyable ones.

As I contemplated my role in materially creating the situations that led to my bankruptcy, I miraculously came to the conclusion that I did indeed create the situation. At the time, I was thinking one-dimensionally, meaning that I was only looking at the actions and decisions that had resulted in the financial problems. But it was a start, and my spirit guides congratulated me on my success. Really? I wasn't interested in facetious remarks from non-incarnate entities.

But they had my ear again, and they persisted in showing me my role in the situation, and how I could just as easily have created a different outcome through different choices. I did create that situation, and I could now create another, through redirecting my choices and actions. After all, who had signed those loans? That makes me a creator within my own life, at the very least on the physical plane or dimension, and in a very direct sense. I could not disagree with that, it seemed quite obvious. They had my attention back, and I began to learn about creation to understand it from a more esoteric level.

Despite having a very successful business, I had begun to worry about bills after buying a new house. Suddenly, perhaps in the space of two months, I lost about a dozen new clients. By entertaining needless worries about money, I had created more opportunities to experience worrying about money. It was an energy that compounded on itself. I created the entire experience myself, and from it I learned about the realities of the creative process on the physical plane, on psychological levels, and in esoteric terms of the creative process. There had been no specific reason for any of those client projects to end when they did. Nothing on the physical plane produced those situations.

On the physical plane we make decisions that affect outcomes. Psychologically, we can allow self-defeating thoughts to interfere with our actions on that physical plane. On the esoteric planes of creation and the Law of Attraction, our energetic state either does or does not bring us the opportunities in the first place. It is those opportunities, and how we create, attract and receive them, that allows us to have the experiences we desire.

What I learned in my situation is that I had a deep-seated desire for a much simpler life, one that afforded more time away from clients and career, for enjoyment and more leisure time with friends. This was not supported by my decision to buy a much larger home – my bills went up, not down, requiring more work, not less.

The Universe understood my request for more free time, more freedom, and less work – and solid clients simply vanished. That seemed to confirm my worst fears, and in a worried psychological state, it was difficult to replace the lost income, and I began to worry more. The Universe responded to that by presenting further financial problems.

Ultimately, one way or another, your deepest desires will be fulfilled – whether you are aware of those desires or not. Now that I have gone through that experience my life is far more peaceful, simpler, and virtually worry-free. I enjoy each day more, and I also appreciate all that I have much more deeply – something that had not really been a focus of mine before.

I am not advocating financial bankruptcy as an enlightening experience upon the spiritual journey. It was how I learned to acknowledge my very active role and responsibility as creator within my life, on various levels. And that realization opened the door to understanding and exploring how I can create more enjoyable experiences for myself instead.

So we begin the discussion of the first step of the creative process – the actual step of creation itself, where we create the opportunity for experiences. This is the step that is the most automatic and we have the least direct influence over – because we create from being. This section is not about actions that we can do, it is about understanding what shapes and influences what we do create for ourselves, how, and why. It requires some clarification on the "being" part of "create from being" – that part of us that Is, regardless of what we "do". For that, we'll be starting that discussion on the outside of the proverbial onion of Self and working our way inward.

Your Thoughts are Not You

Your thoughts are an activity of your mind. Your consciousness observes these thoughts and listens to them, but thoughts are not a product of your consciousness or of your being. In fact, thoughts do not necessarily reflect the viewpoint of your being.

Since thoughts are not part of your being, they do not create. Thoughts are often associated with the creative process however, because they ARE significant to Law of Attraction, which brings your creations to you.

I am discussing thoughts in "Creation" rather than "Attraction" in order to show them as distinct and different from consciousness and being. This distinction is a keystone in understanding how we do and do not affect the creative process.

Where do thoughts come from? Our mind is that part of our brain which "thinks." When we are not focusing our mind upon anything in particular, it tends to respond to events around us along established, learned patterns and personality traits. For example, if someone cuts us off in traffic, someone described as "good natured" might just shrug it off, remembering the last time he/she did the same thing; someone else who considers themselves to be in a bit of a hurry to get someplace might become annoyed, swear, or hit their horn. The good-natured person has quickly forgotten about the incident, while the other is more likely to carry that sense of irritation for much longer.

The thoughts we entertain affect us energetically. In physiological terms, body language certainly reflects our state of mind at any given time. We pick up on obvious body language signs which are displayed facially or by gestures. We know when someone is "in a bad mood" even before they say anything. Their face may look dark and contracted, while someone that is excited has a very bright and open look to their face. The thoughts that have led the subject into their present state of mind is the culprit for the obvious "mood".

Beyond body language, in the same manner, thoughts affect our aura, the electromagnetic field around our body which is continually being generated from our physiological state of mind. It can expand and contract, and it conveys whether we are afraid, compassionate, angry, excited, trusting, or guilty. Intuitives can read auras and see them as a combination of colors.

Why is the aura important? Because the aura connects us magnetically with all that we create for ourselves through the Law of Attraction.

We create far, far more than we ever actually experience. There is a time delay between the act of creating an experience and the physical manifestation of that experience. If there weren't, then stray thoughts or desires would manifest instantly, and few of us would live past our first fearful thought or feeling of panic. For instance, if we looked over the edge of a cliff and for a terrified moment pictured ourselves plunging over the edge, then without a time buffer it would actually happen.

We never experience most of the opportunities we create because we don't attract them into our reality. Our aura is continually changing because we tend to be inconsistent in our thoughts or expectations of life – they tend to waver back and forth. It is the magnetic properties of our aura which attracts the experiences we have created. If our "time delay" passes and our aura has changed, then we never attract that experience we created in a different mood.

It is worthwhile to monitor your own thoughts – but equally important to avoid the double-edged sword of overthinking that very same process! Overthinking often leads to self-judgment or worry, neither of which is constructive along the path of creating joyful experiences.

The first step is to begin OBSERVING your thoughts, without judgment. This alone may take some practice. Instead of being IMMERSED in your daily activities, "watch" yourself during the day and see what thoughts pop into your head, and gauge how each thought FEELS to you. For most this is a fundamental change in approach to daily life. Don't allow yourself to become frustrated with yourself if you find that you keep forgetting to observe your thoughts – because that frustration is a self-judgment. The very word "observe" means simply noticing, without attaching a label of "good" or "bad" to any particular thought. Again, this DOES take practice for most of us. It is a crucial step in simply becoming aware of what is occurring inside our mind.

Once the practice of observing thoughts without judgment has been established, the next step is to begin CHOOSING. Once again, choosing is not judgment – choosing which thoughts to retain does not require labeling them as "good" or "bad". Simply decide how a thought FEELS to you, then either choose to keep it, or choose to replace it with something that is more pleasing to you.

When I first began this process of monitoring my thoughts, I was more than a little surprised at how many self-judging thoughts I had in my head. "You don't know how to do that!" or, "You really screwed that up!" When such a thought appeared and didn't feel good to me, I began to stop and ask myself, "Really? Is that what I believe about myself?" Often I would realize the thought did not in fact match how I felt about myself, and I could physically feel myself lighten up just a little bit each time I confronted and released such thoughts.

The mind does learn through repetition. When we stop to question and release certain thought patterns and ideas, they eventually stop occurring. In time, I began to have a more positive view of myself. We'll talk about self-image more when we discuss beliefs, but for now it's enough to begin monitoring and becoming more consciously aware of thoughts, and to begin intentionally choosing your thoughts, and to recognize them as an activity – not indicative of who you are, and not an activity to judge yourself for.

What Consciousness Is

Psychologists generally consider consciousness to be an awareness of some sort, an awareness of both external experience and of our internal impressions of it. Beyond that basic definition, there is a range of disagreement among philosophers and psychologists about the actual role of consciousness regarding its interaction with our experience through choice, emotion, action, reaction, and thought.

My guides define consciousness in this way:

> *Consciousness is that which observes ALL.*
>
> *Consciousness and Mind are not the same, for Consciousness does not "think". Opinions, attitudes, and judgments do not exist at the level of Consciousness, and so there is no individuation there – it is differences that INDIVIDUALIZE EXPERIENCES.*

Think about that for a moment. To observe is a detached experience, and is an activity which does not interfere with actions, thoughts, judgments or decisions. To observe is simply to be aware of what is occurring. To me, that summarizes the role of the soul.

As a teenager, I had a picture in my head that the human brain is not the physical storage center for all our memories and knowledge, but rather more of an interface to "someplace else" where the actual storage of these memories took place. As an adult in the computer industry, when I considered how much electronic storage it takes to house just an hour of video, which has only two senses (sight and sound) versus our 5, I felt my concept held merit. I do not see how the brain can actually hold even neural-scaled memories for an entire lifetime with five senses, plus emotions – I believe the brain is merely the input / output interface for "offsite storage" of memories.

All human experience is recorded in what many call the Akashic records. All the actions, emotions, perspectives, ideas, experiences and thoughts of each of us, throughout our many lifetimes here, are continually adding to this immense record of humanity. Edgar Cayce referred to it as his source for information, as do many present day psychics or readers. My guides refer to it as the "tapestry of life", and describe it as an intricate work of colors, thoughts, feelings, and patterns. The threads which we as co-creators weave interact and interplay with each other to create new patterns.

Humanity is a dichotomy – we are a human combined with a soul. We are both in one, at once both the immortal soul as well as the mortal human, cooperating in a shared experience.

The soul has incarnated for a specific type of experience in this lifetime. It has chosen a particular body, personality, region of the world, family and friends, and set of talents and predispositions in order to facilitate the chosen experience. So the next time you are angry at a family member or critical of your body or other innate traits, perhaps it would be helpful to consider the possibility that your soul was very specific in this selection, and it may be worthwhile to try and understand why, in relation to the desired experience of this specific lifetime.

Where is the separation, if you will, between the soul and the human? It is my belief that the soul is merely the observer, both in conscious and subconscious states. The human side contains the personality, the ego, and the mind. This is where we consider our experiences, make judgments and decisions about them, and put our next ideas into physical action – as the brain also contains the control centers for the physical body.

In my view, the soul is connected to the body through the central nervous system. This is the ideal point from which to record our entire human experience – for all the senses, emotions, and thoughts occur within the nervous system.

The soul is able to communicate with us as well, and does so through our feelings. We sometimes say that we don't "feel right" about something. To me, that is a message from my soul indicating that particular experience isn't what the soul had in mind and takes me off my soul path through life. In particular, I have come to learn that when I feel a deep seated feeling of restlessness within me, that is an indication to look around and pay closer attention to my actions and decisions. In this view, the central nervous system is actually a physical conduit between the soul and the human body.

Now that we have differentiated between thought, which is an action on the human side of our dichotomy, and consciousness, which is the soul's presence and awareness of our human experience strictly in an observer role with some interaction through feelings, we can begin to discuss the being side of us from which we actually create.

The State of Being

The concept of "being" was initially difficult for me to grasp, but as inferred by the title of this book it plays a core role in the process of creation:

> *Create from being,*
> *express by doing.*

In fact, "being" is not something we need to start doing, we already ARE doing it – we ARE creating and attracting Life experiences based upon our "being".

Being is a state, it is who and what we already are, at this moment. It is how we FEEL about people, things or events, but it is NOT what we THINK about them. Our being-ness is very closely linked to our vibration, our signature which is unique within the Universe, as well as our marker of progress within our own spiritual growth.

We ARE a human being, and we are BEING uniquely ourselves. Whom we are being is a result of all experiences, realizations and self-growth, over all our lifetimes prior to this present moment.

Being is not what we do, but it does shape how we do what we do, and it does influence the choices that we make.

As previously discussed, thoughts also are an activity, something that we do, but not whom we are being. In fact, thoughts do not always represent who we truly are.

We can easily change what we do, and we can train ourselves to think differently. But changing who we are, whom we are being, occurs only through choice, growth and self-realization.

We are not our thoughts. Our thoughts are separate from our being. That was a tough concept for me to grasp initially. I identified with my thoughts, I tend to feel guilt at times and judge myself for my thoughts. But, in reality they are not who I am. In fact, they do not always even reflect my true intentions or beliefs.

What happens when you are NOT thinking? Whether in meditation, or simply very relaxed, when not engaged in thinking, you are still aware – still conscious – of your being. That is sometimes called the observer state. Your thoughts are not evaluating or judging the current experience, merely observing it. This is a very pure state of being, of consciousness, one in which there is no worry or fear – because that is a thought.

> *In the spaces between words, the spaces between thoughts, there is only bliss.*

Who ARE you? That's always an interesting question to ask people. Do you answer that question by giving your name? Your occupation? Your status as a parent? Your nationality? Your favorite sport or hobby? Still, those are activities and labels, they are not who we are.

The state of being requires no activity or thought. You already are who you are, and whom you are being is unique in the Universe.

We often identify more with what we are doing, than celebrating whom we are being. Your being-ness is HOW you choose to do things, when you are choosing by feeling. You might be courageous, timid, playful, kind, or joyful, for example.

Being is how and what we create. Since our state of being IS our vibration, our frequency, it attracts people, things, and events that are LIKE us in some way. That is a great key in the creative process.

My guides have explained this differentiation to me in many different ways over the last few years, but this is the one that finally began to illuminate the concept for me:

> *Our advice is very simple: LIKE yourself; EXPLORE yourself; EXPLORE being ever MORE YOU! How's that? Simple – but VERY effective.*

> *Your being is the unique way in which you view and approach and interact with life.*

Each moment, choose to be in a joyful state. Rise above apparent circumstances, situations and challenges; remember WHO YOU ARE, a child of the Divine. Remember that you are with your body, but you ARE NOT your body. YOU are first, and your body is SECOND; why? Because your body is a creation, at all times, of your inner beingness. What sounds like a riddle is in fact the reality.

Immerse yourself completely in the experience of being YOU.

When we make choices in life, they either do or do not accurately represent who we are. If we made all choices in life based upon how we feel about a situation, instead of what our thoughts say, then we would always be choosing in agreement with who we are.

Consciousness and being are topics that can take some time to grasp and absorb – at least they did for me. It's helpful to understand them, because they are where we create from.

Reigniting Desire

Desire is a crucially important part of the creative process. It shapes the direction our life may go; and it expresses the direction our soul wishes to go.

Desire is a very natural process. It happens automatically. We are born with the propensity to desire certain types of experiences. As children, we are very clear about what we want. We may want to become an astronaut; we may want to watch a favorite cartoon; we may want to go to the amusement park; we may want an ice cream sundae; we may want a huge hug from a favorite relative. We are completely uninhibited about knowing and expressing what we want.

Our desires often mature as we grow. Girls may dream of a fairy tale wedding; boys may dream of flying a jet plane or having a wilderness adventure.

At times life seems to demand pragmatism. We need income to pay for food, a home, and transportation; that seems to take precedence over the safari, the cruise, hobbies, play, and the swimming pool. Often family obligations likewise become a priority over desires. Yet even as adults we need our playtime to remain balanced, and connected with our desires.

In many cases, we allow past disappointments to quell desire. We stop allowing ourselves to want certain experiences that didn't seem to work out the way we expected, or that we don't feel are attainable. We stop imagining the dream wedding, the perfect relationship, the exciting vacation, the fun career. We even squeeze out the hobbies and activities that are fun and playful for us.

It is always worthwhile to remain connected with our desires, to imagine them, to visualize them, and to take the time here and there to do so. The state of life at any given moment does not imply what the next moment, day, month, or year may hold – but yet we tend to believe that it does, and we tend to accept that. In doing so, we limit ourselves.

Desire is a highly magnetic feeling, and it is a fundamental part of the creative process. Desire is pure – it is what we really want, before we start talking ourselves out of believing that we can have it, or that we deserve it, or that it is "possible". It is a request from the soul of an experience the soul wishes to have. True desire is a soul-level message.

Desire is a feeling – not an emotion. It is already within us, for the soul already knows what it would like to create and experience. It is not a reaction to external situations, but the decision to suppress desire to avoid the possibility of disappointment is a reaction and a choice.

> *The higher your vibration, the more quickly do you mani-fest your desires into those experiences which best fulfill them. At the higher vibrations, Dear One, are you also closer to your deepest desires, and so the experiences are more satisfying as well.*

Allow your desires to come to the surface, without wondering how they may happen. Become aware of those times when you are talking yourself out of feeling your desires, and ask yourself why. Release your self-imposed limitations and blockages to simply acknowledging what you want to experience in life. Desire is a message, a request, from the soul, it is part of your being, and it does hold the power to create those experiences for you if you allow it.

Pathways to Dreams

Dream always, and always dream anew: for desire is the beginning of creation.

As children, it seems so much easier to connect with our imaginations and to project fairy tale visions of our future. Sometimes in childhood our daydreams are not easy to separate from material reality, and we readily believe anything is possible. If you don't have dreams for your life, then it will be more difficult to create, attract, recognize, and experience them.

Dreaming is a natural process, one we usually excel at as children. Our imaginations in childhood seem unlimited at times. As adults, it can be much more difficult to reconnect with those dreams, with that imagination. It is far too easy to become boxed in by pragmatism that tells us if we don't have big dreams, then we are less likely to be disappointed if they don't come true.

What are your dreams? And is it possible for you to believe in them? Do you ever take time to imagine yourself emotionally experiencing your dreams?

Interestingly enough, my guides suggest that, for me, the bigger my dreams the better. When my dreams are small, then I begin to mentally try and determine ways that I can physically build up to or create them by doing, instead of creating them from being. When they are very large however, my imagination runs more freely without practical bounds, and I can simply enjoy picturing them without wondering how I can "make" them come true. In that way, I can easily access a truer representation of my dreams, without getting bogged down by the mechanics of HOW they can occur – since that's the job of the creative process.

Are you afraid to daydream as an adult? Often it's because we don't want to be disappointed. The way to dream without disappointment is to release expectations of how and when our dreams will transpire. The point of dreams is to produce experiences which will result in our feeling a particular way.

We just discussed that we create from desire. To disallow desires to surface is to rob ourselves of the experiences they can create in our lives. The creative process is designed to bring us experiences designed to invoke the feelings that we experience associated with our dreams. Just because it doesn't look the way we expected it to when it does show up, doesn't mean that it won't provide the experience of the feeling we wanted.

I think of a dream as a visual roadmap to a desire or a particular feeling – a dream is how we envision or picture ourselves in an experience which produces that feeling.

In the creative process it is useful to consider that when we dream, we are picturing something tangible that is rooted in and based upon esoteric desires. Our dream may involve a nice big house that is paid off, with children and pets playing in the yard, a lucrative work-from-home business shared with our spouse, and a nice cabin cruiser docked out back. We use imagery to feel our desires. The desires behind those images may be to feel the company of a large loving family, the freedom to spend play and work time together, freedom from financial obligation, and a way to enjoy the water. If we allow ourselves, we can create a version of that dream which may look different but will fulfill those desires – probably better than our own picture would have.

Dreams are an embodiment or expression of our desires. They help put us in the feeling of the desires. Even if they don't manifest exactly the way we picture them, we do create the opportunities for the feelings that drive them in the first place.

I once channeled a beautiful message from my guides about dreams. It is one of the most beautiful messages my guides have ever given me, and I hope that you enjoy it as much as I do every time I read it:

> *Of Building Dreams.*
>
> *Of what are dreams built? Desire. Dreams do not spring from will nor intent; rather they ORGANIZE will and intent in order to bring those dreams into physical being.*

48

Know your desires in honesty and in full acceptance. Allow your imagination to create your dreams from pure, unadultered desire. See them clearly, feel them completely.

The rest, the doing, is easy.

When you want those dreams FOR others as well as for yourself, then you have magnetized them, and created a support system to assist in the creating, the doing, the bringing into form and tangiability.

How, then, to "do"? Invite your dreams into daily life. Accept them as a current work in progress. BEGIN to live with your dreams as part of your reality.

How? By FEELING the vibration in your life today which most closely matches the vibration you seek through the realization of your dreams.

Each day you live with full acknowledgment of the similar vibration in your life – that vibration GROWS (within your focus) until it has expanded into a version of your dream.

And here we use the word "version" because the Universe IS creation, is founded UPON creativity, and seeks to delight you always with a UNIQUE version of your dreams. For when you are most clear and honest (with Self) of your desires, then what you are visualizing is your joy upon EXPERIENCING your dreams. Creation is an INTERACTIVE process – there are other energies and consciousnesses involved, and so what is created and presented into your awareness will always BE a more ACCURATE version of your heart and soul's desire than your MIND is able to visualize.

It's rather like Christmas morning – you are HOPING for a new bicycle, but your senses will be excited to discover whether it is blue or orange, what the seat feels like, and how FAST it can go: exploration.

And in the exploration of your creations do you begin to LEARN now about the creative paths of the Universe, and how the DESIGN of the Universe interacts with you directly in the creative process.

This is when one learns the joy of eternity – for it NEVER, NEVER becomes predictable – eternity is an adventure to be savored without end.

EXPLORE your creativity; sing joyfully about your present life, and all that you find pleasant in your everyday experiences – sing from your heart and from your soul. You will continue this path of elation until it is all you can see about you. And all those who are in resonance, and able to remain with you, will experience the same (or rather, THEIR version of it!) For no two experiences ever have been, or ever will be, identical, within the framework of this existing Universe.

You will learn to unite your mind and your heart as one, to share your dreams and desires together. It is in the learning and the mastery of this that creations become faster and more complete.

This is a skill achieved only through creative experimentation.

We challenge you to focus upon the knowingness of SELF: for we can teach and guide, dear one, yet it is YOU as you walk upon the Earth, it is YOU who chooses and creates from desire and from dreams.

So bear this in mind, and begin to explore the divinity WITHIN you – the birthright of Earth humans is the ability to create, and to be fully and completely supported in this endeavor.

Remember at all times that it is YOU who brings creation forth into new forms to be experienced by you and by others.

You have clarity of intent and purity of heart, and these are required for honest creation – meaning, creation of that which you would actually ENJOY the most. For the mind is not always clear nor aware, and yet the heart is heard by the Universe to express most purely the deepest desires of the soul.

For there is an internal process, an automatic one, of the soul's desires passing THROUGH the human body itself, to be created into this reality.

The Earth herself is, through Ascension, creating an ever greater environment for the support of the creativity of humanity.

Be very clear within yourself about WHY you want your desires – this grounds you within the body as the desires are translated through the dimensions into physicality: the human body is DESIGNED as an instrument of creation – to create within this realm and upon your Earth, specifically.

Bring creation forth from your desires, into dreams, through joyful realization of the same already and presently within your life – to conscious realization and enjoyment of the result of creation itself.

You may watch this entire process from start to finish – and you then will begin to realize the creator that you truly are.

We watch in fascination – so many beautiful shapes and colors and textures hover around you – which will you choose? Where will you begin? What will you love into being?

For, ultimately, what you will conclude is that it indeed IS love which IS the creative force in your galaxy, and beyond into the greater Universe.

The greatest joys you will ever experience here will be the combined joys of humankind's growth.

Now go! Choose – bring forth – create – and share what you have learned about the powerful and empowering creative nature of humanity!

The Moment of Now

The moment of Now is the crux of the creative process – for it is the only point in which creation can occur. We create from being, and since that changes as we grow, we create only based upon whom we are at any given moment. Our focus and desires in the present Now moment determine what we are creating for the moments in the near future, and that is why we have discussed topics related to awareness and Self in such depth prior to this topic.

I can remember being in grade school and learning about verbs – the past, present, and future conjugations of them. I clearly recall having some difficulty with the concept of the "present". I understood the concepts of the past and the future very clearly – one had already happened, and the other had not. But I really struggled with the concept of the present – because it just seemed to me that by the time you've completed a thought about the present – it was already in the past. The definition of Now, or the present, seemed elusive to me.

Yet in terms of creation principles, I had it completely backwards. In a sense, the only thing that actually matters or even exists is the Now moment, the present. The past has already occurred, and cannot be changed, and the future cannot be experienced before it arrives in another Now moment.

The past does have value because it led to the realizations, conclusions, and experiences which shaped what we understand and whom we have become in this Now moment. Meanwhile, the future has not yet occurred – because it is in the Now moment that we are creating and attracting the future we will next experience.

So what is the Now? The Now is a moment. It is the ONLY thing that matters – because what happens in any given moment actually creates what the next moment will be. And that Now moment, every moment that passes, holds the potential to change life forever. If we carried that realization with us throughout our waking day, the conscious anticipation would allow us to create amazingly incredible experiences for ourselves.

How long is a moment? A second? Ten seconds? A moment is exactly the length of one breath. When we breathe in and out we are interacting with the creative energies of the Earth, the energies all around us.

The way that we are choosing to perceive our experience, right now, of what we have already created, has an effect on what we create next, as do our thoughts and beliefs, which are always changing and evolving as a result of how we choose to perceive these experiences. It's very much an iterative process.

This explanation from my guides helped me to begin understanding the concept of the Now moment, and its significance, in a practical way:

> *We speak to you now of Patience. For in Patience is God's perfect divine will fulfilled.*
>
> *Patience is focusing on what is NOW, not what is not YET. Patience is focusing on HERE and NOW. For only in this one, present moment is God's Plan unfurled, God's Grace dispensed. Do you see this? It can be the ONLY focus, for nothing else IS.*
>
> *This does not mean, "do not plan." But – plan without losing your FOCUS, your FOOTING, in the NOW.*
>
> *All things are fulfilled in the present. All things exist and appear in the present. All actions and decisions are made in the present. YOU LIVE ONLY in the present. Truly – there is ONLY the present.*
>
> *This is the key to joy, the release from the burdens of life, and its dramas.*
>
> *It takes so much to occupy you! Yet if you understood that the very Universe is recreated anew EACH MOMENT, if you tuned in to what IS all around you, the awe and wonder of Creation would fill your soul like a balloon of joy,*

and you would rise above it all. You would be occupied, overwhelmed, satisfied. You have felt this before. We challenge you to LIVE in it, IMMERSE yourself in it.

FLOW with the tides of life, do not try to DIRECT them.

Expect without NEED, and expect without losing complete focus on the PRESENT. That is grounding. Simply expect, then release.

To ask is to NEED. That is not the way things are. You know all, you are all, you can do all. When you ask, who are you asking? Simply know. And expect. Then release. THIS is how things ARE.

You now live much better within the scope of a day. That is great progress for you. Now, we challenge you to live within the MOMENT. For in each MOMENT is the very next moment CREATED. Time itself is created anew each moment, within that moment!

A moment = a breath. It is creation. True time, the entirety of time, is only a single moment long. It is recreated with each breath. The Universe expands and contracts with its own breath, as does the Earth, as does Man.

To begin bringing your dreams into reality, invite them into your present, not your future. Change your speech to the present tense more often. Instead of saying "Some day I'll find the perfect mate", say "I'm excited about meeting the perfect partner". Bringing your feeling about the future into your experience of the Now will help to create that reality sooner.

Also, keep your conscious focus in the present as much of the time as possible. When wading through the past, or projecting what the future holds, you are not focused in the Now.

The Grand Illusion of Time

We live and operate within perhaps the greatest illusion ever, one that tops anything Hollywood can ever produce – the illusion that we are locked in time.

Time is an illusion with a purpose.

Each day contains 86,400 seconds. Each day is exactly the same length, at least according to a clock. So why do some days seem to drag by, while others seem to fly too quickly for us to keep up?

Time may be a linear construct, but our perception of it, our experience of it, is not. That's because our perception, our experience, is emotion-based. When we are having fun, time seems to "fly". When we are worried about something, or when we dread an upcoming anticipated experience, then time seems to "drag".

Time, or at least our experience of it, is related to resistance. When we resist or avoid something, time seems to slow down for us.

When we try to avoid an experience, it has nothing to do with the experience itself – but rather how we ANTICIPATE that we will FEEL in the experience. There are certain emotions which we don't enjoy. When we avoid an experience that we expect to invoke certain undesired emotions, then we are resisting it – and time seems to slow down for us.

Most of us live on a schedule at least some of the time. We have appointments, deadlines, meetings, and a myriad other activities that involve other people and are time dependent. We rush to avoid rush hour traffic. We rush to catch a bus or a plane so that we don't miss it and have to wait for the next one. We rush to the theater so we don't miss a movie. If we aren't there on time, someone else will be and they might take our place, or we might miss out on something. Rush, rush, rush. We rush to avoid waiting, we rush to avoid rushing. We certainly like to hurry around!

The obvious disadvantage of living in such a harried mode is that our focus tends to be on the next five things we have to do after the thing we are doing right now. Our schedule itself becomes our focus, instead of what is occurring in our present Now moment. That leaves us little room for the conscious enjoyment of the experience we are presently in.

In an earlier career as a project manager, my schedule was sometimes booked five months in advance, and I usually traveled by plane all week long. I knew that missing a single flight could have a ripple effect on weeks' worth of scheduling. I was always on the go, and always under stress – although at the time I believed that I really enjoyed that hectic pace.

When I left the corporate world and ran my own business, I discovered the joy of being able to manage my own schedule. I found that I could set my appointment times during periods which would keep me out of heavy traffic, I could decide which projects to work on depending upon what I felt like doing, and I could leave enough time between appointments to allow me to relax and enjoy client meetings instead of watching the clock. I was more focused on the current experience than worrying about the next one.

I also started choosing travel routes that were more scenic, and I began to notice things I had never taken the time to notice before – parks full of spring blooms, rolling hills, orange groves, kids happily playing, other drivers staging their own personal karaoke event in their cars.

I discovered – much to my surprise – that despite how much I used to rush around, I really enjoyed a relaxed pace much more.

The way in which we are experiencing our lives, moment by moment, has a direct effect upon what we are creating for ourselves. When we are rushed, we are missing out on the opportunity to fully savor and enjoy experiences we've already created, and in doing so we're telling the Universe that we like to rush around more than we like to enjoy our lives, and the Universe responds by co-creating experiences to keep us even busier.

Sometimes in life we don't have the luxury of a relaxed or flexible schedule, but sometimes we also take that schedule a bit too seriously. A busy life does not necessarily preclude us from being able to enjoy the flowers along the way, but it does often take extra focus and attention on our experiences and less focus on the schedule itself.

Later we'll be discussing the importance of HOW we experience, perceive, and enjoy our present Now moment in determining how and what we next create for ourselves. With respect to the creation step of this process, it's enough to realize the importance of where we do place our focus.

A worthwhile focus when consciously exploring the creative process is to recognize your schedule as your own, to take time to do the things you love, to prioritize them, and to set time aside to reflect on the things that you enjoy about each day.

Attraction

Once we have created an opportunity for an experience, we must connect with it in order to experience it. We create many, many opportunities which we never experience. There is an intentional time delay between the events of creating and experiencing what we have created – sort of a safety buffer.

The act of creation itself is somewhat automatic from our perspective, since it is based upon our being, not our thoughts, actions, or other easily modified behaviors.

However, we can influence which created experiences we actually attract into our reality. We do so by being very present, conscious and aware of how we are perceiving and enjoying the experiences in our now moment, and by the choices that we make.

The Law of Attraction is one of the Universal Laws. It is part of the mechanics that runs our Universe. It governs which experiences involving people, events and things we encounter from moment to moment, from among the range of opportunities we have created based upon our state of being.

As implied by its name, the Law of Attraction is a magnetic force. It brings people, things, events, circumstances, and energies together.

Here on Earth, magnetism attracts the "north" or positive pole of one magnet to the "south" or negative pole of another, while the similar polarities repel. We like to say that "opposites attract." The Law of Attraction works in the opposite way, bringing matching energies together. It is based upon vibration. We attract experiences which are a relatively close match for our vibrational rate at any given moment.

We humans generate at all times around us an electro-magnetic field, sometimes called an aura. It is continually shifting and changing in response to many factors including our attitude.

Think of your aura in this Now moment as a balloon, and your vibrational rate as helium. The higher your vibration, the more helium you have infused into your balloon, and the higher you go. Let's say that you are having a great day, and that you are feeling very happy, secure and purposeful about life and yourself. Your balloon fills with helium and you float up to about 500 feet. From moment to moment, as wind currents in your life breeze past you with brief experiences that cause you to slightly raise or lower your vibration as your mood and attitude fluctuate in response, you may bob up and down a few feet here and there. But you stay at basically the same altitude, and in doing so, you encounter the balloons of other people who are at the same vibrational rate.

Now let's say you have an encounter with someone which causes you to feel inferior – perhaps your boss drew an error to your attention and you were scolded. You "deflate" just a bit, you lose a little bit of helium as your self-confidence deflates just a little, and you dip down to 450 feet altitude. While in this vibration, at this altitude, you will encounter experiences with a vibration that is at this level – experiences which will seem to confirm how you are feeling about yourself at the moment, and match that mood.

Happily, how we perceive events in our lives, and how we think about them, is a choice. We have already discussed the experience of being human. In not allowing the boss' scolding to cause us to think that we are incompetent, in not taking it personally, our vibration stays up and we continue to have a good day marked with pleasant events anyways.

It is easy, fun and enjoyable to work with the Law of Attraction and see its results in daily life. This section will provide insights about how to attract more enjoyable experiences into your Now – experiences which you have already created for yourself.

Managing Emotions

Thinking about my dog, I once asked my guides if pets have emotions.

Sure they do! They just don't get emotional about them.

Animals experience emotional reactions to situations just like us – then they move on. By contrast, we humans tend to experience our emotions, then begin to think about them and rehash them, often building up a huge protracted emotional experience from what in reality was merely a single event.

We tend to experience our lives emotionally, then reflect upon them mentally. Emotions are a part of our physiology, and therefore they are a built-in part of the experience of being a human. They are how we experience life.

Certain emotions are considered unequivocably enjoyable, while others are not. Yet both are part of life, and it is because of the lows that the highs can be so thrilling. It is this emotional aspect for which we as souls line up lifetime after lifetime to return to Earth as a human.

Life IS an emotional journey. When we find ourselves avoiding a particular situation, what we are really avoiding is the way we anticipate that we will feel in that situation. I usually find that the procrastination itself is usually far worse than the actual situation.

Denying emotions, or ignoring them, or avoiding the situations that we fear could be emotionally unpleasant, is resistance. Resistance tends to build up in the physical body and create illness if repressed for long periods. We are here to experience life through those emotions, and to learn and grow through emotional experiences, so if we stop that process then our reason for being alive and being here begins to wane, often taking our health with it.

We attract specific experiences because of what we will learn from them. They tend to follow us through life until confronted. A popular saying advises that when we run away from a situation, we take our problems with us. That is very true. If learning to stand up for ourselves is something that our soul intends, then we may find ourselves in a job situation with an overly demanding supervisor. If we are afraid to confront the boss, then we may quit the job, only to land in a relationship with a pushy partner. In my own life, I find that the situations become more and more extreme until I finally choose to react differently and begin standing up for myself. Then, suddenly, I no longer attract that kind of situation, and I find myself in a difference cycle to learn something else.

It is in facing our individual fears face on that we will gain the most from life. It's often said that we have nothing to fear but fear itself. Fear can be crippling. But it is in tough times, when we MUST work through our fears and act, that we learn to work with our emotions instead of letting them drive our lives.

The Moon is often associated with our emotional side, and is a point of consciousness just as people, plants and animals are. I once channeled the Moon, and emotions turned out to be the topic.

> *I am Selene. I am the voice of that which you call your Moon. In a sense I truly AM "your" Moon, because I came here just for you.*
>
> *I have not always been with your Earth. Eons ago, it became understood that your emotional body would need a cycle to help regulate its evolution. The solar day is too short, the solar year is too long. I was happy to volunteer to accompany you on this journey.*
>
> *I have watched your great civilizations rise and fall, come and go. But I have RECORDED every emotion, during every lifetime, that you have spent upon your Earth. The human experience upon Earth is an individual journey. Lifetime after lifetime, as you gaze upon me, I reflect your own emotions back to you. I see you differently than you see yourself, because I see you at this moment as the culmination of all the lives you have ever lived.*

I create the tides of your oceans. Your own body is mostly water, and in the same way I impulse your emotional body through cycles of growth. The only way to grow through emotions is to face them, and I mirror them back to you for that reason. Do you remember me from generations ago? I remember you! I have not changed much, but my how you have grown!

I am not interested in your great civilizations, because growth upon your Earth as a human is an individual journey. And it is individuals who create and destroy civilizations. All begins with the individual. When you look within is when you experience your greatest revelations. And at those moments I reflect to you those emotions that best suit your own introspection.

I play with you in the astral planes of your Earth. Have you noticed me in your dreams? How do you feel when you look up and see me on a moonlit night? Do you feel our bond? We have an intimate relationship, you and I, and I am here for you, as I was during your very first experience upon your Earth.

I provide the perfect balance for you and the Sun. I impulse you to seek the perfect balance within your own life. Every time there is an eclipse, I am the perfect size to hide the Sun. The eclipse is how we remind you of the importance of balance, and that it can be achieved.

You may tune in to me to help with emotional times in your life. I am always here, and I can best help you when you are the most honest about what you are feeling. Do not judge your emotions; do not deny them. I know all your hopes and fears; your dreams and disappointments; and I do not judge you. I merely record and remind.

Every full Moon, face east and watch me rise as the Sun sets. If you are truly open, I will reflect your emotions back to you. Feel them, love them, let them be expressed.

Laugh. Cry. Scream. Sing. Curse. Release. When you are that open, I will guide you. Afterwards, you may notice that I look slightly different to you – because I am reflecting different emotions, a renewed you.

City lights have changed your daily schedules in present times, and you are less observant of my cycles. This has impeded your emotional evolution, from my perspective. If you are ready for emotional growth – call upon me.

You humans love to marvel at your achievements. Many of you love to worship Creator. If only you could see that you are all creators, and that the greatest thing you will ever create is YOURSELF.

I am Selene, and I enjoy every moment of our journey together.

Feelings Come From Within

Feelings are not the same as emotions, but they are closely connected.

Emotions are a physiological event within the body in reaction to a situation. Emotions include surprise, rage, sadness, grief, gratitude, and embarrassment, among others. Chemicals are released into our bodies as we experience events, in reaction to them, and that creates the emotion. Emotions are primarily in the body, in response to outside stimuli.

Feelings are the opposite in that they come from within. We determine how we feel at any given moment based upon our beliefs about ourselves and our relationship to what is happening within our lives.

We commonly hear, "he/she hurt my feelings!" That statement is not only inaccurate, it is impossible. Our feelings reside within us, and we own them. They are connected to our beliefs about ourselves. It would be more accurate to say that someone has made a comment which triggered our own self-judgment of some aspect of ourselves. In that way we have decided or chosen that our feelings are hurt, because we have not addressed and released the underlying belief that we are inadequate in some way.

For example, if we don't feel or believe that we are attractive, and someone makes a comment about our appearance, that self-judgment is triggered. We are only affected because we are being reminded that we feel inferior somehow in the looks department. If, however, we feel or believe that we are great at chess, and someone criticizes our chess game strategy, then the comment would not bother us, and we would not experience anything emotionally – because we don't believe it, we don't agree.

People will emotionally react differently to the same situation because their beliefs about themselves are different. Ultimately our emotional reactions always reveal what we believe most deeply about ourselves. Things that bother us are triggering deeper beliefs about ourselves, areas in which we retain self-judgments.

Emotions are momentary. Once the initial physiological reaction has happened within the body, it is not sustained. However, we humans are very good at frequently recalling experiences that we considered emotionally painful, and in doing so we are adept at RE-CREATING the way we felt at that moment. In this case it is a combination of the memory of the event, and the belief or self-judgment, which re-create that emotion within the body.

I have learned that when I am surprised by my own reaction to a situation – if an unkind comment hits home with me, I stop and ask myself whether I really do believe that about myself. I confront it with honesty, within myself. If I discover that I have a judgmental belief about myself, I address that. Other times, I find that I have already healed or released such a belief, but that I am still repeating an emotional reaction by habit – then I can easily confront and release it.

Feelings exist at a deeper level than emotions. Feelings include desire, joy, happiness, peace, curiosity, and love. Feelings can also help us to make decisions – a choice may "feel good" or "not feel good" to us – that is an internal "GPS" system of sorts. Feelings are how we connect with our intuition, or soul.

The importance of feelings in the creative process is that they reveal underlying beliefs that are affecting what we actually create and attract. It is common to have beliefs of which we are unaware for long periods of time – beliefs which prevent us from having experiences we want. These feelings are most easily revealed through emotional reactions to situations.

We only attract that which we believe we deserve, or believe we can have, or believe is possible. So our feelings can help to reveal what we may or may not believe.

My guides have often emphasized with me the importance of being "emotionally open" when seeking spiritual growth and awareness. I interpreted that as being emotionally reactive at all times, so they clarified:

> *Staying emotionally open does not mean "being emotional all the time": it means being AWARE of your FEELINGS about the people and events in your NOW. And so we*

suggest – release your THOUGHTS, and locate your FEELINGS.

How we are feeling about life from moment to moment plays a very key role in determining what opportunities we actually attract to us. The more consistently we maintain the feeling we wish for life to provide us - excitement, joy, freedom, comfort, security – the easier and more quickly we will attract the opportunities that will support or increase that feeling.

Happiness is Innate

If you believe you are not happy, it is because you have chosen that belief.

Happiness is not a choice, but being unhappy is. I would like to suggest that we are innately happy until we talk ourselves out of it by perceiving ourselves and life experiences in certain ways which we judge to be undesirable. I believe that we are already happy, that it is the natural state of a human being to be happy, and that it actually takes energy to be unhappy, because we must create the illusion of unhappiness and we must sustain it – it is not innate.

We often seek happiness outside ourselves, or as a result of experiences. We say that we will be happy if we get a certain job, or if we win the lottery, or if we locate the ideal mate. Yet happiness is a feeling, a state of being, so we can only experience it within ourselves. It is not an emotion, so it is not even connected to the external world at all, so experiences cannot produce it. Winning the lottery can certainly provide opportunities for enjoyable experiences, but none of those experiences can reach inside and make us happy if we have already decided that we are unhappy.

Happiness is not something that can be sought or located, because it is not outside ourselves and will never be provided by the outside world. It is something to recognize or realize, something that is already there, inside, if we clear away and release any obstructions that block it.

We think we are unhappy if we choose to focus upon what we don't have, instead of appreciating what we do have. And in such a case we are certainly likely to create and attract experiences which will seem to confirm that life is an unhappy experience for us, since that is where we are placing our focus.

Happiness is an innate state of being for humanity. It's already there. So if it's our natural state, and emotions generated by outside influences cannot affect happiness since it is a feeling and not an emotion, then why do some say that they are unhappy? What can cause a disconnection from happiness? Judgment, which is a result of thoughts.

My guides like to say that we are already happy, until we talk ourselves out of it. To be unhappy is a decision at some level, although not necessarily a conscious decision. To say that you are unhappy because of events or circumstances in your life is not true. To say that you have decided or chosen to be unhappy because you would prefer your life be different is more accurate. At any moment you could make a different choice and feel the happiness again.

In fact, since happiness is our natural state of being as humans, it is actually work to be otherwise.

> *What could be simpler than BEING happy each moment? It requires energy, focus, effort to be otherwise – as happiness is your natural state of BEING.*
>
> *Your state of BEING at all times is a CHOICE, whether you are conscious of it or not.*
>
> *When you are not drawn into external situations, the joy and peace are free to flow from within.*

To undo the decision to be unhappy, to stop allowing life situations to convince you that you are not or cannot be happy, will dramatically change what you attract into your life. A happy person attracts experiences that reflect his or her own happiness. It doesn't work the other way around. If we aren't already in recognition of and experiencing our own happiness, then we will attract situations that confirm our illusion of or choice of unhappiness. Waiting for life to make you happy will never happen, and is unnecessary. It's completely within your own control to feel happiness.

Anytime you think that you are unhappy, ask yourself why. It is one thing to honestly acknowledge that you are not enjoying a particular situation or aspect in your life. We are human, we have emotions, and we encounter situations in life which we don't particularly enjoy. However, it is an entirely different thing to convince yourself that you are "unhappy" because of it.

When we decide that we are unhappy "because of" something, we are establishing a belief based on judgment rooted in emotion and generated by thought. And when we are in the focus of the belief that we are unhappy, can you guess what we are creating for ourselves? Experiences to confirm that we think we are unhappy. We are sending the Universe a very clear message that says "I believe I am unhappy because I didn't enjoy that situation. Please send me more situations in which I am likely to feel like this – more of the same, please!"

This is simple and straightforward. To exercise your choice to remain happy is a step towards greater emotional control over your own life. I asked my guides for an exercise that would illustrate this section. They simply suggested that I tell readers to start reminding themselves more often that, beneath the self-constructed layers, they already ARE happy – it's already there ... just SAY it more often. "I am happy."

Addressing your relationship with happiness within yourself will create change within your life through the attraction of different kinds of experiences – experiences that will reflect this state of happiness to you.

Choosing Joy

Joy is not the same as happiness – joy is happiness in motion or action. While happiness is a state of being, joy is HOW we experience or act within situations. Happiness is a peaceful realization of life, while joy contains an enthusiasm for experiencing What Already Is, and excited anticipation for What Is Yet To Come. Joy has an anticipatory aspect – we get excited about what we expect to happen. It is accumulative, and expansive – joy creates joy.

Recognizing and experiencing joy in life is a decision, a choice. And it's a very important one in the creative process. This is a very frequent topic from my guides. Creating from within joy is a new paradigm which human-ity as a collective whole is currently integrating.

> *A path chosen in joy is an exponential path indeed. For joy creates joy, which creates joy, and so forth. A joyful ex-perience is created ONLY in a joyful state – which creates an even MORE joyful experience. This is the truth and the heart of Ascension.*

> *We have said before that increased self-enjoyment would usher new joys into the life, and it is so now with you. For joy begins within – is shared with and into the world – and returns in greater measure and in new, resonant forms.*

Any experience can be found to have a joyful aspect. Choosing to experience even the smallest facets of life in a joyful way will have profound effects on creating more joyful experiences for us. Whenever I feel that I'm doing something I feel obligated to do, I stop myself and find some challenge, or some new way of going about that task, that will make it fun – like a game. Joy can be found in the most unlikely places!

Joy is found in the en-joy-ment of life. That's not just a play on words. Since everything in your life has been created by and attracted by you, enjoying the experiencing of it sends the Universe the powerful message that you like to be in the state of joy – and we get "more of the same".

Energy always travels in a circular pattern, and always returns to its source in greater measure. When we project a joyful attitude, we are creating an energy movement and sending it out into the Universe – and it will be returned to us.

Take time to find excitement or joy throughout the day, in all that you do, and you will begin to notice a change in the overall tone of your life.

Recognizing Your Belief Systems

We each carry a unique set of beliefs that we have built up throughout our lives. They shape our actions, decisions and choices in a profound way. We often are unaware of just how deeply these beliefs run, and how directly and completely they drive our lives.

> *What Is is merely a reflection of what you believe that you deserve, and what you believe that you can have. Replace Seek with Expect; replace Want and Need with Desire. Look forward to each moment that arrives, knowing that it contains bread crumbs on your trail to the future of your greatest choosing.*

There are level of beliefs embedded within us, beliefs we have collected over our many lifetimes. The outermost level of beliefs we hold are those involving what is likely to happen in the world around us. The innermost beliefs, the core beliefs, are those which describe how we view ourselves, what we can or cannot do, and what we deserve from life.

The most important beliefs that you have, with respect to the creative process, are the innermost beliefs, the beliefs about yourself – not beliefs about external events, laws, rules, deities, or religions. If you do not believe that you deserve to have a certain experience – that you are unworthy in some way – then you will not attract that opportunity, even if you have already created it for yourself.

Our beliefs are not part of our being, they are not part of who we are. They are a layer, a framework, which we build up that can cloud our understanding of who we really are. They are called beliefs because we have come to believe them over time. Through life experiences, we evaluate what occurs in our lives and we draw conclusions from those evaluations which shape future expectations and actions. Sometimes this is a conscious process, but most of the time it is subconscious.

If we go to several job interviews without securing a job, for example, we may begin to develop the belief that we are not qualified or experienced enough to get a job that we want. That is a belief, an assumption, a result of thought, and it is very likely that it will affect our ongoing job search. We may start aiming for lesser positions than we really want, thinking that we cannot have what we really want. We may begin to carry an intimidated attitude into an interview for a job that we do want, leaving the interviewer less-than-impressed. In that way we are permitting a belief to interfere with what we allow into our reality.

"If you touch that fire, you'll get burned." At some point, usually early in life, most of us tried to touch that fire, and sure enough, we burned a finger or two, and we labeled that an unpleasant experience. Yet there are those who walk across glowing coals and embers without burning their bare feet. What if they had been our parents? What if we were raised to believe that fire can be safely experienced without pain or harm if it is respected? Would we still have burned those fingers? Or did we burn the fingers only because we were told it would happen, and we believed it?

On a more esoteric level, beliefs about what life is or is not able or likely to offer us prevents us from having the vibrational match in order to draw those opportunities that we most want to us through the Law of Attraction.

If we believe strongly enough that something will happen in our lives, it probably will, because we will attract it. Whether on a physical, or subconscious, or esoteric level, we are very likely to experience situations that we consider to be inevitable.

It is impossible to lie to the Universe regarding the creative process. The Universe does not listen to our words or thoughts. The Universe reads our feelings and our beliefs, and notices how much time we spend with a particular focus, and what emotion we have during that focus. That is how the Universe shapes energy into the experiences that we create and attract.

Fortunately, just because you think or say something doesn't mean you really believe it. Your feelings are the best gauge for your true beliefs. Sometimes I have a thought or judgment about myself or my life, one that surprises me. At such times I stop and ask myself, "Really? Is that really what I believe?" Usually I am quickly able to realize it was simply a fear-based thought or worry that doesn't fit what I actually believe about myself.

However, there are times I do realize I have the image of some shortcoming of mine. I take the time to work with those as they arise, to identify those self-judgments as something to confront and release.

It is worthwhile to acknowledge our beliefs about ourselves, because they cannot be swept under the proverbial rug, since we ARE the rug. When a limiting belief about ourselves comes to our awareness, it is an opportunity to examine and release that belief. Because when we have limiting beliefs, we are telling the Universe that we don't believe we are good enough, capable enough, or worthy enough for certain opportunities and experiences, and so we will not attract them into our reality.

In much the same way, we often hold limiting beliefs about life – what is or is not possible. Since our beliefs about life are usually based upon our experiences, we tend to draw conclusions based upon our own past. "I never win anything!" or, "Accidents always seem to happen to me!" or, "My car breaks down at the worst times!" or, "People always say bad things about me behind my back!" or, "Every time I take a vacation it rains!"

My guides' comment on this topic is simple, clear, and very much to the point:

>	*What you believe, will be.*

It is completely unnecessary to make assumptions about the future based upon the past, because we are continually creating the future. If we allow ourselves to retain such belief systems, then we will automatically attract experiences which will reinforce them.

Listen closely to what you think and say. When a belief or assumption about life pops up, one that does not support the expectation of enjoyable experiences ahead, then it may be worthwhile to stop and examine why you believe that. At some point, you created the assumption which led to every belief you had, and it is within your power to change it.

Usually it's helpful to recall the past experiences which led to the assumptions in the first place. In our past, there is some disappointment from a prior experience which we don't want to feel again, so we begin to expect the worst for the future, hoping deep down that we'll actually be pleasantly surprised. Unfortunately creation doesn't work that way.

We can revisit, review and release the emotion of past disappointment. We can remind ourselves that there was a specific reason things happened in the past, and that reason doesn't necessarily apply to the future. When I really want to resolve a past event that's affecting me in the Now, I try to understand why things didn't meet my expectations in the past, and why I decided that I was disappointed about the experience.

Changing a belief is not the same as changing a thought pattern, because a belief becomes deeply engrained deep within us and can mask how we actually feel. We can't simply tell ourselves that we no longer believe something about life or about ourselves, we really have to change the way we view the situation.

Limiting beliefs are usually fear-based, meaning that we are afraid of being disappointed. In the case of limiting beliefs about life, we don't want to hope for something that may not occur. When having limiting beliefs about ourselves, we don't want to feel inadequate, so we simply don't put ourselves in situations where we may perceive that we fail at something.

> *Fear is not a feeling, it is a belief that generates emotion.*
> *Beliefs can be changed, and this is how fears are released.*

If we can remember why we are here, that we are experiencing a life as a human, and release expectations of ourselves and of the future, and simply view life as a set of experiences without judging them as success/failure or good/bad, then it becomes easier to release the emotional bonds that retain limiting belief systems.

The process of releasing limited beliefs is not an instantaneous one, but it does get easier the more we use it. And, ultimately, it will allow us to attract more expansive and more enjoyable opportunities and experiences in our futures.

One idea that might help you to begin changing your view of yourself is to begin a habit of complimenting yourself – for how you look, for a kind deed you performed for someone, for trying something new whether it worked out your way or not. I have found over the last two years that I held so many expectations for myself, that I was always more focused on what I didn't complete or accomplish, instead of praising myself for everything that

I did, and everything that I attempted. You can also congratulate yourself for simply making a decision whether to do or not do something, because our choices are very important to the creative process. You could even begin to thank yourself for things that are already in your life, since you created those too! I have found this technique can truly be an effective way to change your focus, and eventually your beliefs, about yourself. Over time, as your positive thoughts about yourself increase, there is less and less room for limiting beliefs, and they disappear.

Messages in Mirrors

Mirrors help us to see ourselves more clearly – they provide reflect for introspection.

As we have discussed, the Law of Attraction is a magnetic force which draws people and circumstances to us which have some similarities to us.

A natural by-product of the Law of Attraction is that we end up surrounded by mirrors. In saying 'mirror' I am referring to someone or something that reflects back to us some trait or traits which we have, so that we can examine it externally to ourselves. The purpose is that it can be much easier to notice something external to us in order to contemplate it introspectively.

It seems we tend to have a bit of a blind spot at times when it comes to ourselves, and since the spiritual journey is about completely accepting and loving the Self first, the Law of Attraction serves to offer us these mirrors. This is an opportunity to see our traits displayed externally so that we can decide which to choose and retain ourselves.

I noticed something odd among friends and acquaintances some time ago: I began to notice that whatever complaint they stated most quickly, most often, and most loudly about other people, was more often than not something they themselves did, said, or resembled. Eventually I realized the same thing about myself. More often than not, when I am uncomfortable with an action or aspect of someone else, I find it's because I have a related self-judgment.

Last year I found myself frequently becoming irritated with an indecisive friend, who seemingly took forever making commitments and decisions. Eventually when I questioned my reaction to this friend, I realized that it was my own hesitation and indecision in life that was really bothering me – the friend was only the mirror.

When you begin to notice patterns in your life, experiences that trigger an emotional response on your part that says you don't enjoy the experience, take the time to acknowledge that you have attracted the situation and determine why. It's not always easy to see ourselves objectively, and that's the exact reason for mirrors.

Even when we can see ourselves objectively, it's not always easy to be honest with ourselves about those behaviors or characteristics we display which we don't want to admit we have.

Mirrors do provide an excellent and accurate reflection of ourselves, and in doing so they guide us to the aspects of ourselves which are attracting the experiences in life we are not enjoying.

The Importance of Attitude

Nothing determines what we attract into our experience of life at any given moment more than our attitude. Without getting esoteric about it, that just makes common sense. It can be observed on a physical level, a psychological level, or on deeper esoteric levels.

Attitude is a vibration, and it is magnetic. When we are in a "bad mood", we are far more likely to attract unpleasant experiences and to encounter other people also in a similar mood, and certainly to experience them in that way.

Attitude is not contagious, but it is very suggestive. Try walking through the mall or grocery store, beaming a friendly smile at strangers who look like they are having a rough day. Notice how quickly most people will respond in kind.

It is very helpful to the attraction process to become aware of and monitor our attitude throughout each day. I find that I can accumulate a bad mood without being immediately aware of it.

How do you structure your day? How do you choose what to do first? The tasks or situations to which we give the highest priority, and the attitude with which we enter each task or situation, has a large effect on our vibrational rate throughout the day, and consequently affects what we create to experience later.

My guides like to advise me to find the "joyful aspects" of anything I do, and to make that my focus. In fact, if I cannot find a "joyful aspect" of a particular task, their advice is to come back to it later when I can approach it with a good attitude.

Why is attitude so important? Our attitude is a large component in attracting into our experience that which we have previously created for ourselves. We tend to accumulate an attitude during the day – meaning that if we enjoy what we are involved in for a longer period of time, then we are far more likely to be in a better mood, and are thus better prepared to not get upset when something doesn't go our way. The reverse is equally true.

Most of us have a variety of things we "need" to do on given days – errands such as banking or shopping, personal or business appointments, shuttling children to and from school and activities, and going to work. Many of these activities are at set times which gives structure to the rest of our day, and often we find ourselves "squeezing in" the less time-constrained activities and tasks. Many of those other tasks may have time-specific deadlines as well, but generally during the course of any day we do make many, many decisions about the order in which to arrange and complete those tasks.

So how can they be prioritized, and why is it helpful to do so? I suggest prioritizing them by beginning with the ones that you would enjoy the most, the ones that appeal to you most, first. As just discussed, this is more likely to make it easier for you to remain in a better attitude as you approach those things you are less eager to do. This can provide a very different experience and make it far easier to enjoy them.

Additionally, prioritizing your day by those things which you would most enjoy has the esoteric effect of raising your vibrational level, and since the Law of Attraction is a magnetic force, you will be far more likely to attract more pleasant experiences to you.

The Law of Attraction brings us a match for our vibration, often reflected by our mood and our actions and attitude towards others, at any given time. It not only brings us the experiences we desire and enjoy, it also brings experiences we don't enjoy, particularly if that is the energy we are creating and spreading into our environment, and infusing into the aura we carry with us.

The mere practice of arranging our day around the things we WANT to do first because we would ENJOY them more places our focus upon the enjoyment aspects of what we are doing.

However, I should stress that this technique can be undermined if it becomes a way to avoid less pleasant tasks we are putting off or resisting, because in that case we are prolonging our emotional resistance to something we don't want to do, and that does put a damper on our vibrational level because it is avoidance.

We often have things to do on a daily basis that we would prefer not to do. Can you, in honesty, find something that you WOULD enjoy about those tasks? Can you make them into some kind of a little game? Can you challenge yourself to find a way to make them more interesting, or perhaps find a more efficient way to do them? That would be your best option, vibrationally speaking. If not, then suck it up and get it over with as quickly as possible to free yourself up to do something which you CAN find enjoyment in. That would be better than spending a longer period of time resisting that you must eventually get to it.

The Power of Focus

About a year ago, I was very much occupied with my freelance website business, but it wasn't producing enough extra money at the time to allow me to take a break, and I was very much wanting a vacation. I chose a vacation anyways, and started picturing it. I decided that I would begin setting money aside for it, even if that meant I would have to tighten spending in other areas.. I marked an envelope "vacation" and put $50 inside to get it started. I began getting excited about it and picturing the vacation. I set the intention that I would take that vacation, even though I wasn't yet sure where the money would come from. I decided that I deserved the vacation and it was time to begin planning it.

Within three days, seemingly out of the blue, I received two large client projects, both of which involved travel, and an additional free airline ticket. These surprises not only provided more than enough money to take the vacation I wanted without neglecting other things, but I was able to extend the vacation.

That was my first intentional experience with conscious creation, and I am still amazed at the synchronicities. What I learned about the creation process from that experience is that when I choose a direction and focus on it, and beginning pre-emptively planning for it, without allowing worry to interfere, the Universe is more than capable of supporting my desires.

In today's fast-paced society, we don't always take the time to really focus on what we want, because we can be so busy simply trying to "keep up" with life. Yet the process of creating really does mandate that we know what we want, spend time picturing and expecting it, and believe that it will happen. Here is a message I channeled regarding the role of focus in the creation process:

> *Be aware at all times of your current focus, and watch what that brings you. Your cycles of creation are shorter now because you have raised your own vibration.*

What is your present focus? What is your greatest desire? Do you love your desires? Do you nourish and feed them? In doing so, you give them LIFE.

Choose intentionally and remain consistent. The fewer desires within your focus, the more quickly they can and will be created.

At all times, be aware of these desires, and be sure they are not perceived as needs.

When they arrive, embrace them fully and enthusiastically. Love them.

Be very clear about your desires. Dream from an esoteric place, towards an emotional result.

When your reactive emotion upon the appearance of your own creation closely matches your ANTICIPATED emotion, then the Universe responds to this CONSISTENCY with "more of the same".

Love your creations, even if you choose to RELEASE them afterwards. Never dispose of your creations! Cherish or gift them; never discard.

See all experiences as learning, see NONE as failures. Be grateful for ALL that the Universe produces in response to your wishes.

Celebrate each gift – then, choose or do-not-choose it.

Always choose based upon your own desire for fulfillment. For example, if you desire something for another, then focus upon how YOU will feel upon providing that to another, NOT upon how your RECIPIENT will feel. Do not take this journey outside of yourself, because you can truly create only for YOURSELF to GIVE to another for your OWN JOY, should you so choose.

Always begin with the spiritual, for that is what and who you truly are. Let the physical be manifested from the spiritual to support you with all that you desire.

No thing is too great or too small.

We further suggest you devote more TIME to SELF-ENJOYMENT without reservation or guilt. That vibration will expand and create more quickly than any other, for that is the highest physical expression of self-love.

Transformation begins within: transformation of self, transformation of your environment.

The Universe awaits!

Receiving

We've discussed how we create and attract opportunities and experiences involving people, events, and things into our lives. How we actually receive and experience our own creations is the most conscious part of the process, and is significant in how we create and attract in the future. It provides a feedback loop of sorts, informing the Universe how well the creation matched our desires – based upon how we enjoy it.

The receiving aspect is the most conscious activity for the entire process of creation. We continually create, because that is who and what we are. We do it continuously and automatically. While my prior discussions provide useful insight about how it works, your creations will only change as your vibration changes through soul growth.

We are likewise continually attracting that which we have already created, yet we do not receive the majority of what we create. Life is filled with opportunities, all of which we have created. In fact, there are always more opportunities than we can receive or experience, thanks to the existence of time. This is intentional, and it necessitates choice. It is through our choices that we grow and refine our realization of what we truly enjoy, and also through our choices (and how we receive them) that the Universe refines how it co-creates with us.

I would say that the process of receiving that which we have created and attracted goes something like this:
- Recognize the opportunities
- Choose (or, do-not-choose)
- Appreciate & enjoy what we have chosen to experience

The Universe likes to offer a variety of opportunities for expansion in the form of different choices in response to our creative activity. Opportunities often will not look exactly as we may have pictured, and this is because the Universe has a deeper and more clear understanding of our soul's desire which initiated the creation in the first place.

We usually do not recognize all the opportunities that are presented because they don't match what we expect to see. Sometimes at least one of the choices will be familiar so that it's easier to recognize, but not always. This is where awareness becomes valuable. The more opportunities for a given situation that we can recognize, the more we have to choose from. It is very rare that there is but a single way to follow your path through life. The choices presented exist to offer us varying levels or options for growth. We may choose any of them or none of them.

Often making a choice that is more of a risk, or takes us beyond our "comfort zone", provides the greatest opportunity for self-growth and realization.

When we recognize choices in life, choices which we have created, one way to choose is by feeling. When we picture ourselves in each situation, which feels best to us, and why? Does the mind agree or is it arguing with the heart? My guides always advise that I choose with the heart, bring the mind into agreement, and allow the mind to enact the decision.

Being "open to receive" begins with an open heart. How do we know our heart is open to receive, and what does that mean? If you simply focus upon your heart as being already open, you will feel more love within you, more love for self, which is where all love truly begins.

If you begin experimenting with this, and there are areas in which you actually don't love yourself, they will come to the surface. You will find situations begin to occur within your life that help you to become aware of areas in which you could accept and love yourself a bit more. For me, these situations were in the form of challenges. I attracted experiences with people who tried to convince me I was not deserving, not good enough, not worthy of having an enjoyable life. At first this was very frustrating for me. Finally I simply began one day to focus more upon loving myself, and liking who I am, regardless of what others seemed to believe about me. My life immediately changed for the better.

The process of receiving begins with the heart – because we must love ourselves enough to consider ourselves worthy and deserving of what we have created in order to recognize and receive it. In other words, we must be "open to receive" – as described by my guides in this message:

Opening to Receive ...

... begins within – at the heart center.

First, love yourself enough to ALLOW good things, with the complete realization that you are deserving.

Second, love others enough to permit them the JOY of participating in your life, through the SHARING of THEIR joy with YOU.

See all gifts in the light of the joy in which they are presented.

A gift may be a word of encouragement; or it may be a new car; or it may be a million dollars. A gift is measured by the joy it transmits. A gift always begins from the heart, and returns to the heart, of the giver.

When you offer any gift, from your heart to another, feel the joy of giving. Feel this within your own heart.

Allow yourself to RECEIVE any joy or appreciation that is offered in return. Know that this appreciation may be offered at the soul level, beyond your immediate perception. Be open to accept this joy in whatever form it may materialize within your life.

In this way, you have opened your heart to receive.

Are there any questions?

[what about that million dollars comment?]

It was a creative suggestion; and also a reminder that measuring gifts in different "sizes" is a limiting thought. If you can picture yourself giving something TO another – then you should also be able to picture yourself RECEIVING that same gift FROM another.

Giving in joy ALWAYS returns to the giver, whether or not you perceive that. The return may not be obvious, but we assure you that it occurs. Always. Joy is energy. Energy always returns to source. It is your CHOICE whether or not to RECEIVE it.

And does that clarify?

[yes ... thank you.]

It is our joy to have given you this.

How we receive and experience an opportunity is the subject of this next section. The following topics offer perspectives on how to consciously participate in the receiving process.

Expectations Create Tunnel Vision

Expectations are a very common pattern of thinking for us – we believe that we must have a picture of how a situation should turn out if all goes as planned. In fact, we can get downright specific about how, when, and where we fully expect something to occur – and who else we expect to be involved, and how. Yet the Universe loves to challenge us to hold broader perspectives and awarenesses when observing what actually occurs, and why.

Expectations usually limit our experiencing of a situation. They lead to tunnel vision, and often judgment. When things don't go as expected, then we often judge that something has failed. The greater truth of the matter is that everything always works perfectly – when we have the clarity to properly interpret the outcomes of a situation. The disconnect is usually in our limited thinking about what the exact outcome should be.

The ultimate way to trust in Life is to simply follow your heart and do those things which most appeal to you, without an expectation for exactly what will transpire next. However, we live in an extremely structured society which expects us to form plans to reach specific goals as a measure of success.

What we can do is relax our expectations regarding the SPECIFICS of how we think something will turn out – and when they don't match, have the patience to attempt to understand why.

Relaxing our expectations certainly helps us to recognize a broader range of opportunities as they arrive into our awareness for choosing, thus apparently broadening our options in life.

As we receive our own created opportunities into our lives and experience them, similarly relaxing expectations helps us to enjoy the experience we are having, even if it doesn't precisely match how we pictured it.

More often than not we are creating from essences – we are creating experiences in which we will feel a certain way. Building up pictures with many specifics is very helpful to the creative process, but is not always exactly how the Universe will present the scenario to us.

At the receiving stage of the creative process, opening our minds broadens our awareness, and helps us to recognize more of the opportunities which we have already created and attracted for ourselves.

Limitations Are Self-Imposed

We all place limitations upon our lives without even being aware of it. Since we create our own realities, it is usually ourselves, not others, who are limiting the kinds of experiences that are created and attracted into our lives. Limitations stem from our beliefs about ourselves and what we believe is possible within our lives. Fortunately there is a very simple way to learn what we really believe about what we can and cannot do, or what is and is not possible.

Nearly twenty years ago, a friend once commented to me that he thought I was a negative person. I took that very personally, and at the same time I strongly disagreed with his assessment of my personality. For the first time in my life I began to LISTEN to myself, and notice exactly what I did say, and evaluate how that might sound to others at face value. I was surprised to realize that he was correct. I had a very strong tendency to focus on the downside of a situation instead of seeing the upside aspects or possibilities.

That realization bothered me deeply, and I began to review the entirety of situations before commenting or developing an opinion. I began to look at all sides of a situation in order to determine which felt best to me. If the first aspect that jumped out at me did not feel good to me, I would stop and ask myself if I really believed the thought, and whether the thought was a constructive one or not.

What I was really doing was setting up a process to compare my thoughts to my innermost feelings, and over time I found that all my initial thoughts became more positive. It was certainly not an overnight accomplishment, and at times when life feels more difficult to me my old tendencies surface and I have to dust that technique off again.

What does that have to do with conscious creation principles? Do mere words that we utter have the power to create unpleasant experiences? Fortunately, by themselves they do not have that power. They do, however, very much reveal to us what we believe is or is not possible, and our beliefs can prevent us from attracting enjoyable experiences, thus limiting us from experiencing all the joyful experiences we may have created for ourselves. If we don't believe something is possible, we will not attract that experience into our lives.

If you have never done it before, I encourage you to begin paying attention to exactly what you say, and reviewing it. A compact digital audio recorder might be useful for this. Do you find yourself saying things like, "I'm just no good at tennis!" or, "Sure, I bought a raffle ticket, but I doubt I'll win, since I never win anything." Or, "He won't ask me out – he doesn't even know I exist!" Most of us make comments similar to this throughout the day.

Do these comments reflect how you really feel about your tennis ability, or your luck, or your ability to appeal to someone? Be very honest with yourself. Any thoughts or comments in which you limit yourself will show you how you are limiting your experience of life.

If you don't consider yourself to be good at tennis, do you want to be better? Then perhaps you could say "I'm still improving my tennis game." It leaves open the possibility that more practice would be beneficial to enjoying tennis more, and also leaves you open to attracting more positive tennis experiences, if that's what you want. Or maybe you're simply not interested in tennis. Do you need to criticize yourself in order to express that? Perhaps you could instead say something like, "Tennis is OK, but I really prefer golf." You are replacing the self-limitation with an acknowledgment of a skill you are proud of, and in doing so you are creating a magnetic attraction for some enjoyable golf experiences.

Perhaps you have never won anything at a raffle before, but that doesn't mean that you won't. There is no luck or chance in this Universe. Everything functions in alignment with Universal Laws. Would you LIKE to win the top prize, say a big-screen flat panel hi-def TV? Then don't limit yourself by saying that you won't. Instead, try saying something like, "Yes I bought a raffle ticket, and the football game is going to look great on that huge TV in my family room!" Taking the step of visualizing what you want is very helpful to the creative process. Do not be disappointed if it doesn't always work exactly the way you want it – after all, we're all human and we are here learning how all this works – and for most of us it's very much a learning process!

And, do you really believe you can't attract a compatible relationship among the six billion people on this planet? Do you believe that no one could love you, or that you are undeserving somehow of love? If so, then you may attract a relationship that reinforces that belief.

The point is that we aren't going to attract an experience that we don't believe is possible. The great truth of the matter is that ANYTHING is possible, so why do we limit ourselves?

Limitations often stem from fear of being disappointed. We don't like looking forward to something and having it turn out differently than expected. We have already discussed expectations and how they limit our experience. But with limitations, we aren't even allowing ourselves to create an experience for ourselves, because we've convinced ourselves that it doesn't really exist within the realm of possibility.

I suggest that we call limitations "self-limitations", because we willingly decide them within ourselves, or we adopt them from what others say to us. Guides have the ability to see the true limitlessness of our creative abilities here on Earth, and to see how we limit that with our thoughts and beliefs; here are a few comments they have made recently to me on this topic:

> *The potential, and please listen closely here, the POTENTIAL within ANY given moment throughout the day to DRAMATICALLY change (improve) any situation is UNLIMITED!!! KNOW THIS for it IS SO; KNOW THIS and it SHALL BE DEMONSTRATED to you.*

> *CREATIVITY: this is the challenge now before you. You shall see that the more CREATIVELY you approach life, the greater and more immediate the results. For in order to grow beyond your current limitations, you must EXPAND your VISIONS of what is possible. Show the courage to be PLAYFUL about life, and you will find your magnetism increases.*

> *For you can create a "simple" synchronicity just as easily as you can create a million dollars. There is no difference except in the mind, where all your limitations and barriers exist.*

How, then, to release these self-limitations in order to receive greater potentials into our lives? The first necessary step is to become aware of these thoughts and beliefs. Confronting them in honesty will determine what we truly do and do not believe about ourselves, or about what is and is not possible in our lives.

Our beliefs are a result of our thoughts. Our feelings contain the real truth. We can't just tell ourselves that we no longer believe something. We can't just say "that flame will not burn my finger" and expect to withdraw the finger from the flame unscathed, if in fact we believe differently. Beliefs have to be unraveled, sometimes in steps and layers. For those who can connect with their true, deep, soul-level feelings, it may be possible to release unsupportive belief systems by asking our feelings about the truth of a matter. Or, we can create opportunities to challenge and dispel belief systems.

Discovering and releasing self-limiting thoughts, and the belief systems we have created that support them, is an on-going process. When we make it a conscious focus to do so, Life will present opportunities to assist us.

As we discover and release self-limiting thoughts and beliefs, it is also helpful to replace them with reinforcing thoughts or experiences. If you try the exercise of choosing to see the upside of every situation – perhaps even making a game of it within yourself – and challenging yourself to begin speaking in a more supportive, optimistic manner of yourself and your life – then you WILL begin to feel differently about Self and about Life, and you WILL begin to attract and recognize more enjoyable experiences to reinforce that belief.

Removing Judgments from Choosing

While it is very common for we humans to have judgments, they are not necessary to the process of choosing or making decisions. Holding judgments can, in fact, work against us in the creative process.

Let's define judgment as the labeling of something as "bad" or "good". Most of us make judgments about things throughout the day. When we make a judgment, we generate an attitude about that particular subject. That energy leaves us and goes out into the environment around us.

If you pay close attention, you can actually feel your energy change when you think of something you like and consider "good", then stop and think of something that you dislike or consider "bad". This change in energy does affect the aura, and does affect the creation-attraction process.

There is a significant energetic difference between simply not-choosing something, and judging it. For example, consider the difference between saying "Bobby is an idiot!" and "Bobby and I don't have much in common so we don't hang out." Which remark feels better to say? Which would you prefer someone say when discussing you?

Judgment commonly becomes a habit, and we are often unaware how often during the day we place judgments. We are surrounded by judgment in the media and other people around us in the workplace, neighborhood, school, or shopping center, so it can easily feel like a society "norm".

It is necessary for us to make choices, many of them, throughout the course of each day. Choices ARE a crucial part of the creative process, for it informs the Universe what it is that we prefer, and each choice we make contributes toward the creation of our own future. In some way we must evaluate how something feels to us in order to make a decision or choice.

Choices occur in the heart; judgments occur in the mind. We often combine or confuse the two. The heart chooses immediately and we can sense this choice in our feelings – we either want to do something, or we do not want to do it. Then the mind jumps in and begins to analyze WHY we are deciding in this way and evaluates the choice. That is when judgments appear.

And judgments, like so many other thoughts, build and accumulate. If we had an experience in the past which we judged as "bad", then experiences which we perceive to be similar will also be anticipated to turn out in a similar manner. Such assumptions can unnecessarily taint our experience of the future, and limit our expansion into new varieties of experiences in life.

An alternative to labeling a person, experience, or thing as "bad" is to consider it unsuitable for yourself. Just because we don't choose it for ourselves doesn't make it "bad". We are part of All That Is – which certainly includes anything that we might judge in a negative manner. So calling something "bad" is, in some perspective, no different than calling ourselves "bad".

It takes disciplined practice to notice when we issue judgments, which is certainly a prerequisite to changing that behavior. It is a worthwhile pursuit, however. When we re-train ourselves to relax those judgments, our energy fields actually become lighter and more positive, because we are no longer creating as many lower-vibrational thoughts. Ultimately, of course, this attracts a more positive overall experience of life.

We may judge people, things or events. When we are judging people, that includes ourselves. In fact, very often the aspects of others that we view in a negative light are a reflection of some part of our own character that we don't readily see, as discussed in the section on mirroring.

When we judge things or events by labeling them as unpleasant, it is useful to recall that in some way we have created and attracted those things or events into our lives. What message are we sending out into the Universe then? We are saying that we are successful creators but that we don't create and attract things that we like, and the Universe is more likely to continue sending us those creations which we don't enjoy, because we are giving them our emotional focus.

Any way we look at it, there is no positive outcome within the creative process for holding judgments. Removing judgment from the receiving phase of the creative process may take time and discipline, but will pay off in providing more enjoyable experiences in life.

The Abundance of Opportunities

Life is full of opportunities, but we tend to miss most of them because they don't appear the way that we expect them to, or because we hold back due to fear. That is not a failure on our part, since we are here for the learning.

There is no shortage of opportunity. The Universe is continually presenting us with them. When we begin to become aware of the great many choices we continually make throughout the day, then it becomes easier to begin identifying the great number of opportunities we are choosing from.

If life ever feels stagnant for you, it isn't because there aren't opportunities, it's because you haven't yet recognized and addressed the ones before you still awaiting your choice. It is in the recognition of opportunities that we often miss out.

We also tend to identify "opportunity" as a chance to attend a fun event, or take a vacation, or earn more money. But Life offers us a myriad of more subtle opportunities throughout the day which we don't notice – the opportunity to feel good about letting someone in front of us on the freeway so that they don't miss their exit; the opportunity to take a moment to listen and offer a kind word in support when a colleague at work is down; the opportunity to enjoy the fresh air outdoors. This morning I went out to get coffee and returned to find I had locked myself out. My roommate was gone for a few hours so I instantly realized that my plans for the morning had just changed. I looked around me. After a week of rain this was the first clear, bright day without clouds, so I decided to drive to the beach. I had a wonderful, relaxing morning enjoyed the waves and the breezes, and doing something I don't often do – relaxing. I chose not to get stressed about all the work I had planned to do, since my computer was locked inside. As it turned out, everything did get done on time. Instead of judging myself for being careless about the keys, I instead recognized an opportunity to do something different – relax at the beach.

You have successfully created and attracted every opportunity that presents itself to you today, every opportunity to make a choice, but you will miss or ignore most of those opportunities – because we are always still learning.

If you are desiring change in life, if life feels stagnant to you, then look about you and begin making conscious choices to accept change. Open your closet and wear something very different. Get your morning coffee from a different shop on the way to the office, and enjoy the difference in flavor. Take a different route home, a more scenic one, even if it's longer, and enjoy the new sights. Begin to deliberately make different choices throughout the day, in a very conscious manner, and try new ideas wherever you have a tendency for repetition. These seemingly little choices add up very quickly and have a surprisingly powerful effect on you magnetically. Because what you are doing is sending the Universe a very, very clear message that you are ready for and desiring change in your life, and the opportunities for change will build into greater and greater opportunities for change. You are also showing recognition and appreciation to the universe for all the options for variety that are already available in your life. Doing this exercise for even a short period will quickly and dramatically change how you feel about your life, and what opportunities next appear in your life. It is also a very empowering exercise, as you begin to see and acknowledge how many opportunities there really are in any given hour of any day.

It is our responsibility to be diligent in following up on opportunities. Consider each opportunity of which you become aware – then, either choose or do-not-choose it, but do not judge any opportunity in a negative way; for you have successfully created and attracted this opportunity, and it is important to always honor your own creations. If you successfully recognize an opportunity which you have created and attracted, and decide to not choose it, then it may be worthwhile to take time to understand how you created something that didn't quite match what you really wanted. Where did you place your focus in order to create this opportunity? By evaluating that it becomes easier to understand the creation process.

Becoming Conscious of Choices

Always choose by feeling, and always choose joy.

Life is navigated by the choices that we make. We make them continually throughout any given day. Some seem large, others seem small. Which car to buy? Write with blue or black ink? This job offer or that one? Toss the jacket on the sofa or hang it up? Stay together or break up? Have lunch alone or invite a friend along?

We make so many choices that often we are not very conscious of the decision making process, or even that we are deciding. In fact, nearly everything we do is a choice. There are very few instances during any given day in which we are actually forced to do anything, although we often like to say "he/she made me do that!" More often than not when we say that, it isn't really accurate. We make our own choice in almost any given situation.

Even our attitude at any given moment is a choice. Someone might provoke us a little, and push our buttons, but whether we respond in anger or not is entirely within our own control – it is a choice. It may not feel like it – but we do in fact control our emotions, not the other way around.

If you disagree with this, look more deeply into your own reactions to occurrences throughout the day. There are likely few, if any, instances in which we are truly forced against our will to do something – there is usually a choice involved, although sometimes we feel trapped or obligated.

Perhaps a manager at work demands that you do something you don't feel right about, with the implication that your job depends on it, and you comply. In that case, you made the decision that the job was more important than your preference in the matter. You were not truly forced to do anything against your will – you made the choice.

Recognizing all opportunities for choice is absolutely essential to understanding and accepting the extent and responsibility of your own choices in the creative process. We are not often aware of the number of decisions we make during any given day because we have closed ourselves off to other alternatives, so the decisions we make are often automatic, whether we like the outcome or not.

The choices we make, and the attitude with which we step into our choices, is important at the receiving end of the creation process. When we make a choice, we are accepting an opportunity we have created for ourselves. We connect with that experience and it becomes a part of our reality. The way in which we react to that experience, and whether or not we appreciate and enjoy the experience, affects the kinds of opportunities we will create and attract to us in the future.

> *Once you have decided the priorities for the experiences you desire, then focus upon them with the same priority. In this way are your mind and your heart UNITED in the creation of, and attraction of, and recognition of, those experiences.*

Simply being more present and aware throughout each day – being very conscious and intentional about recognizing and making small and large choices as they arise – can be very empowering.

Appreciation is an Action

Appreciation of What Already Is will increase your vibration more quickly than any other state of being. For when you are appreciating What Already Is, you are telling the Universe that your own creations are good, and in this raising of your vibration do you begin to attract other experiences which will provide you with a similar or greater feeling of satisfaction with Life.

How, then, to fully appreciate? My guides suggest that saying "Thanks" is one-dimensional. Real appreciation is an action verb. To truly appreciate an experience, fully focus your attention upon savoring it.

Full appreciation of any experience has the power to not only raise our vibration instantaneously, but it also places all our focus completely within the Now moment, and in a very positive sense. We are not worried about something in the future, and we are not scolding ourselves for something that is already in the past, when we are truly immersed in the experience of enjoyment.

The pace at which we sometimes consume life experiences in today's fast-paced society often does not lend itself to a full enjoyment or appreciation of most experiences, for we are seldom focused completely upon the enjoyment of a single experience. We are often still thinking about events that happened earlier in the day, or planning what we intend to do next. All we are focused upon is the state of being busy.

The more time we devote to the enjoyment and appreciation of, and immersion in, a particular experience is significant in the amount our vibration increases, and thereby influences what experiences we attract to ourselves next.

Understanding

True understanding comes from experimenting with the principles of creation in your own life.

The preceding sections have discussed how we, as humans beings, fulfill our birthright on planet Earth – to co-create.

By experimenting with and exploring the process of creating within our own lives, we become ever more conscious of how we are creating all that we experience. Being conscious of the process allows us to continually improve our ability to create more joyful and expansive experiences within our lives.

One of the first things that I had to learn was patience. At first I was impatient with the Universe, when things didn't happen in the way and timing that I expected. Then I realized I had to turn that around – I had to exercise patience with myself. When I finally accepted and understood that I truly do create everything in my life, I had to take responsibility for it all myself. I had to begin being patient with myself, in the realization that I had to learn to understand how it all works, and that I had quite a learning curve ahead – one that I was fully and completely responsible for.

Over forty years of life I had built layers and layers of beliefs, judgments, and self-limiting thoughts, far more complex that I could have imagined. Each time I accused the Universe of malfunctioning and not delivering what I thought I had intended to create, the Universe was merely showing me yet another belief, judgment, or self-limiting thought which prevented me from experiencing what I WANTED. The Universe faithfully and accurately offers me that which I create – it's my own understanding that sometimes cannot grasp why I don't have the kinds of experiences I hope for.

I have learned that life is a process of self-discovery through learning to create. When I create an experience that delights me, and I can trace back to see how I indeed created, attracted and received the experience, it is very exciting. And when I experience something that I don't particularly enjoy, often I can likewise see how I created that as well. Either way, I learn something about myself. When I don't enjoy an experience, I look for the belief or judgment that got in the way of allowing the experience I really wanted.

At the rate I'm going, sometimes I think I could be in this learning mode for quite awhile! I'm glad that I have learned to be patient with myself, because there are far more layers to me than I ever would have expected. But with time and experience it does get easier to get the feeling for how it all works. And life does become more and more joyful, because even in unpleasant situations it can be exhilarating to reach an understanding of how I created a particular experience, because then I can ensure I'm less likely to create it again! Realizing the way to end patterns of unpleasant experiences in life can indeed be a joyful experience, even in the midst of the un-enjoyable experience that produces that realization!

Four years ago, my guides told me that eventually I would realize that love is the answer to everything. Now I can understand what they meant. Deep down, in each of us, beneath the layers of all the beliefs and judgments created from fear and pain, we all want the same things – love and acceptance. Through the process of experiencing that which we create, spanning untold lifetimes, we will eventually tire of experiencing situations in which we do not feel loved and accepted. When we see behaviors mirrored back to us from others that we don't enjoy, we eventually decide to change those behaviors within ourselves one by one, lifetime after lifetime. We continually grow and evolve, raising our own vibration, until eventually we become love, and since we create that which we are, we experience only situations in which we feel loved and accepted.

A few years ago, my guides offered the following definition of the "Divine Plan". I groaned and rolled my eyes as I dutifully journaled it, thinking to myself, "here we go with more of that new age stuff again!". Now I am beginning to understand the awesome truth in its simplicity:

> *Divine Plan: that it is impossible by design for all consciousness to NOT return to love, always.*

That sums it all up – ultimately that is the journey we are all on in this merry go round of mirrors, experiences, desires, dreams, hopes, disappointments, dramas, fears, and joys – the emotional roller coaster of being human. We all, as souls, eventually trim and polish off all the rough edges until only a perfect, glistening gem is left – the beauty of love.

As the joy in the process of conscious creation grows within your own life, and as you become more aware and conscious of the process, there are a few additional areas you might begin to contemplate as you strive for a greater experiential understanding of the creative process you exercise in your own life. I have included my understanding of a few of those topics next.

An Intentional Environment

Embedded into our physical environment are representations of what we believe about ourselves, and what we value in life. If we are proud of an accomplishment, we have that degree on the wall in a nice frame, or that trophy openly displayed in a prominent place. If our family and friends are very important to us, we have pictures of them all around us. If we love having guests, then we keep our homes always clean and tidy with refreshments always stocked. If we are very closely connected with our dogs, then we may not worry about repairing the frayed rug that reminds us of their playful puppy days.

There are also elements of our past within our environment – and the emotions related to those past experiences. A souvenir from a vacation spent unhappily arguing with a former partner may bring up the reminders of a stressful breakup, just as easily as a different souvenir may remind us of a fantastic, fun vacation taken with friends. What we place around us from past experiences will usually have an emotion connected with it. It is worthwhile to only keep momentos that are uplifting around us. There is a connection between mood and vibration, and hence which creations we attract into our experience.

Make deliberate changes in your environment that remind you of the feeling you are wanting to experience or increase within your life. Choose elements for your environment that are supportive to creating more fun and joy in your life. If a particular picture or other momento from the past brings a smile to your face due to its connection with happy memories, then locate it someplace where you are likely to see it often.

The idea of "vision boards" is popular these days, and for good reason. If you have a desire for a particular experience, for example a trip to Machu Picchu, and you want to create the opportunity to go there, put a few pictures of it up in your environment, and don't allow yourself to worry about how you will be able to afford the trip, and don't get too fixated on a specific timing – don't limit the Universe. After some time of seeing those pictures every day, you may find that you simply begin to expect that trip opportunity will come up, and your focus will help you to create it, if you are being honest within yourself of any conflicting beliefs that may prevent you from believing that you can attract it.

Having music that you enjoy as a part of your environment is also great for the creative process. Music is a great mood elevator. But another benefit to music is that while we are enjoying music we are often in more of a heart space than a mind space. The mind is where we tend to generate our self-limiting thoughts, worries and fears, which can lower our vibration and interfere with our ability to attract enjoyable experiences. We are also more in the Now and less likely to be thinking about worries while enjoying music.

I recently visited a friend's house, a really gorgeous place. As he led me on a tour through it, instead of just focusing on all the beautiful remodeling he had done, he spent most of the time pointing out all the things he saw as needing to be done. He was setting the energy of something always needing to be done – then was surprised that he began to have a string of bizarre plumbing and electrical issues. His focus was telling the Universe that there was always something that needed to be done on the house, and the Universe provided him with more of that experience.

Have you noticed how you feel when entering a friend's house? Do you find that when visiting a cheerful friend's house, even if they are not present, the energy of happiness is there anyways? Or if you have a friend that is scattered, disorganized, and has a somewhat chaotic life, you begin to feel that way when you get in their car or enter their home?

The way in which we view our space – whether it be our car, apartment, house, tent, treehouse, office, or wherever you spend most of your time, sets an energy field up. If we tend to focus on problem areas, we are most likely to create additional problems that reinforce those perceived problem areas. It is worthwhile to pay attention to your attitude towards your living space, your working space, or your car. If you find yourself commenting to friends that it seems like your car is always needing some expensive repair, or that it is unreliable, you are likely to create experiences that reinforce that belief. Alternately if you focus on how much you enjoy driving your car, and how reliable it is, you are more likely to propagate that experience.

The way in which changes manifest into our environment are as much a reflection of our inner state as friends are mirrors to us of our own being. My car speaks to me. Some time ago both front blinkers went out just days apart. I asked my guides why that happened. They explained that I didn't feel I have a strong direction in my life at the time, and I didn't feel I really knew where I was going with my life, and my car reflected that back to me – blinkers represent direction.

It's worthwhile to regularly review how you feel about everything in your space, what your attitude towards it is, and how it supports you in the process of creating an enjoyable life for yourself, and how it speaks back to you.

Synchronicities Light the Way

We are intimately connected to all that we experience in our immediate environment as being external to us. In some way, on some level, we have created and attracted all elements that we see around us.

Synchronicities speak to us from media, the animal kingdom, conversations, numbers on the clock – the list literally doesn't end. There is no such thing as a coincidence. We create synchronicities in order to draw our attention to something we may not have otherwise noticed. As you explore conscious creation, it is helpful to become more aware of synchronicities and to explore their meaning on a deeper level.

Synchronicities generally occur together in a short time frame, and in relation to a specific situation. Nothing is random, and our environment is a reflection of us and of what we are presently creating and attracting. Sometimes when I pay closer attention to what is happening and when, I quickly realize that my day is full of synchronicities which largely go unnoticed.

They may be subtle, but they add up quickly, and they hold a message. I remember being out and driving my car one day through an area I was unfamiliar with, when the thought of an old friend drifted into my head. Moments later, I passed a street sign bearing his last name, thinking "well now that's interesting", casually to myself. Then just seconds later one of my friends riding in the car brought up in conversation mention of another friend who shared the same first name as the friend that had come to my mind. As I began to really wonder about these apparent coincidences, I passed a delivery truck also bearing his last name. The confluence of those synchronicities kept him securely in the forefront of my mind, and as soon as I got home I called him, only to find that he had just had an emergency – and I was able to calm him down and talk him through it.

Synchronicities can also show us what we are creating and attracting. When I turn my focus to something that I would like to create, such as a dinner out with friends, I tend to notice the names of restaurants popping up around me as suggestions of different places we could go, or the names of specific friends may pop up around me, and I may call those friends only to find out their prior dinner plans were just cancelled, leaving them open.

Noticing synchronicities in radio songs, billboards, comments from strangers, even TV commercials can be a fun game. They can help to illustrate exactly how connected we really are with our own environments.

When noticing synchronicities, it is useful to remember they are not necessarily showing us what we "should" be doing, since there is no such thing. They are, however, an excellent opportunity for us to become more aware of how the Universe is hearing us, what we are creating – in a sense, what opportunities are unfolding for us. This gives us a checkpoint to check in with our feelings and determine whether or not that matches what we really want.

Money Is Just a Substitute

The topic of money probably occupies more focus than most other topics on our minds throughout any given day. Wealth certainly seems to be the primary focus of most discussions regarding the Law of Attraction. Yet money is only one example of energy we attract, and one way in which things can be accomplished. Money also becomes one of the more common reasons for limiting ourselves.

There is a subtle – but very significant – difference between wanting money, and feeling that we lack enough of it. Most of us, most of the time, when thinking about money, are thinking that we need more of it for some reason or purpose. Or, we are thinking that we cannot do something until we have more money. And when we are thinking that, we are not focused upon money but upon the belief that we lack having enough money, and we are very likely to create experiences that support that notion. We are also believing that we cannot attract certain experiences until we have the funds to pay for it, and in this way we push those opportunities into the future which never arrives.

Money cannot buy us happiness, although it can afford us some pretty fun experiences. And when we desire having enough of it to be able to have those experiences, it's really the feeling of that experience itself we wish to achieve. Focusing our creative intentions on that feeling, instead of wondering where the money will come from to pay for it, allows the Universe to suggest ways that it can happen.

Few topics limit our creative activities as much as the topic of money. All too often we allow money to become a barrier in the creative process, through our thoughts and beliefs. We often let go of many of our dreams because we think we will not be able to afford them. We talk ourselves out of picturing experiences which we really do want, because we don't know where the money will come from.

Instead, if we were to simply focus on the image of enjoying that vacation to Hawai'i, living in a more spacious house, or taking scuba diving lessons –

whatever your dreams may be – the Universe can produce the opportunities for experiences to happen which would give us the feeling we seek in wanting those experiences.

We can be so mentally tied to the limiting thoughts of money and prices that we can overlook other forms of support and opportunities when they arrive. If we instead simply focus on what it is that we would like to experience, the Universe is fully and completely capable of delivering that experience to us.

If you find yourself becoming frustrated because you don't see the opportunities and experiences you believe that you are creating for yourself, then examine whether you are really focused only upon the enjoyment of the experience you are picturing, or whether you are doubtful or worried about how you will be able to afford it. As we discussed earlier, beliefs must be in alignment with our creative desires, or we will not create and attract what we really want. If we hold the belief that we won't really be able to have an experience because we won't be able to afford it, then we are very unlikely to connect with the experience we desire.

Being self-employed, my income can vary dramatically from month to month. During trying times, I have truly learned the difference between a "want" and a "need". Whenever the topic of money pops into my head, if it is in a worry or fear context, I immediately turn my attention instead to appreciation for what I do have – health, friends, happiness, peace, and joy; and I also look in appreciation at the material things I already do have. Sometimes we can be so focused on money that we fail to notice and appreciate all the good things in our lives.

There is nothing about money itself that interferes with the creative process. In fact it is an integral part of how our society operates. We can't ignore the fact that we have bills, need groceries, and so on.

Money itself is just the smokescreen, the means to an end, one way in which we can produce a particular experience we desire. Focusing not on money itself, but on the experiences we wish to have in life, puts us in a more direct connection with our own creative process.

What Karma is Not

Karma is very often seen as a punitive or retributive force, bringing bad or good circumstances inevitably back to those who initiated some action for or against another. We often hear of "karmic debt" or "karmic goodwill", depending upon the circumstances. It is commonly considered to be a cosmic force, an inescapable destiny, that follows us through lifetimes until we have fully experienced whatever it is that we originally actioned.

In my perspective, karma is one interpretation of the Law of Attraction. Energy does travel in a circular pattern, and whatever energy we do send out eventually returns to us. When we are helpful to others in good intention and joy, we do eventually reap that back, provided that we are open to receiving it. When we make the choice to affect the life of another in some harmful way, that energy also does return to us.

Where I tend to disagree with traditional views of "karmic debt" is that I don't see it as a punishment for something "bad" we did in the past. There is no such thing as judgment in the higher dimensions, so there is no punishment to be administered. Everything is experience, and that is the reason for creation.

Say that you choose to betray a friend's trust in some way. You have made a choice, and that choice has formed an energy through that particular situation. That energy went out into the Universe, and the Universe came to an understanding that you like betrayal, and at some point you find yourself in a situation in which you are betrayed by a friend. It probably will be a different friend, and a different situation – the Universe loves to answer our co-creative requests with variety.

This friend's betraying action is a mirror for you, to see the other side or role in a betrayal-themed situation, and you created and attracted the situation to you through your vibration. For you never would have made the choice to betray the first friend unless your vibration allowed it. This is how energy travels in circles.

Now let's say you become indignant or angry with the second friend, the one who betrayed you. Your vibration does not change, there is no growth. Another friend or confidant also betrays you in some different way; then another. You are experiencing a karmic pattern.

Finally, one day, instead of becoming angry with the person who is currently betraying you, you suddenly say to yourself, "That really doesn't feel good to me – I am going to make sure that I never betray the trust of a friend like that person has done with me!"

In that very moment, the soul grows a bit. And in doing so, your vibration changes, and suddenly these betrayal scenarios evaporate from your life and stop appearing. It isn't that you paid back some karmic debt until the Universe was satisfied that you had suffered enough for an action you did in the past. You simply changed your own vibration through growth – growth achieved by a simple realization and decision – and now you no longer create or attract experiences of the vibration of betrayal. You personally begin to find that the thought of betraying a friend's trust is very distasteful to you.

We are here to experience being ourselves through our interactions with others. The co-creative process provides a variety of mirrors to reflect back to us whom we are being at any given point in our lives, and as we grow and change whom we are being, then our life, relationships, and experiences will change as well.

Understanding this, and living in very conscious awareness of the creative power behind our decisions and actions, can be very empowering. Seeing our ability to change our own lives, rather than thinking we are somehow victimized by an outside force against which we are powerless, allows us to embrace what we all deserve – a more joyful life.

Acceptance of All That Is

Much earlier we discussed resistance. It seems to me that the opposite of resistance is acceptance. Resistance is a very human thing, and when we resist something we are trying to avoid an emotion we anticipate we will encounter if we allow a particular situation to unfold. Resistance is a behavior that is built up from experiences from which we have formed the beliefs that certain experiences are undesirable or will not feel good to us.

Resistance is a choice, while acceptance is simply the lack of resisting. Resistance takes effort, and we experience unpleasant emotion when attempting to avoid an anticipated emotion. Acceptance is a state of being, a very natural one. It is how we already are, if we are not creating resistance.

When we resist a situation, we are emotionally focused on the resistance of the situation we mean to resist. The Universe feels our focus on resistance, and since that is our focus, produces similar situations which we would want to resist.

When we have begun to become consciously aware of our resistances in life, we can address and confront them. We can begin to unravel the belief systems and thoughts that drive resistances. As we peel away these layers, we begin to discover more and more acceptance to be a natural occurrence with us. We become more accepting of people and experiences. Eventually we discover that we can relax into this acceptance, because as we lower our defense mechanisms (which don't really work anyway), we begin to attract only safe and enjoyable experiences, and our belief that life can be trusted becomes reinforced through our own experiences.

The more acceptance we demonstrate in life, the more we attract accepting experiences to us.

Love Begins With Self

What IS love? Now, there's an age-old question, and one that certainly elicits a wide range of answers!

Is it the giddy feeling that makes it difficult to speak without stuttering on your first date as a teenager? Is it the comraderie and support you feel with your guy friends, or the soft affection and tenderness you feel towards your girl friends? Is it the heady rush you feel as you begin a sexual encounter? Is it the heart-melting warmth you feel looking into a puppy's eyes? Is it the difficulty you feel in keeping a stern parental face as you scold an errant child? Is it the heart-wrenching loss you feel when a close friend or relative has died? Is it the feeling you experience when you give your own coat to a homeless person on a cold night and their face lights up in gratitude? Is it all of these, or perhaps none of these?

It's my belief that love is the natural state of a human being, the innate part of us which connects us with All That Is. The human side of us often learns through unpleasant experiences to be wary of love, for fear that it will not be returned or, worse, will be abused. We humans are certainly not fond of feeling vulnerable. This is a resistance we often build up over time – we don't trust that it is "safe" to love. I don't believe that we are here on Earth to learn to love, because it's already built-in to our nature. Perhaps it would be more accurate to say that we are here to learn to have the courage to love in fearful or seemingly adverse situations.

There is a pattern to love, one that did surprise me when they first presented it:

1. *Love for Self*
2. *Love for Others*
3. *Love from Others*

What surprised me most was that Love for Self was #1. Growing up in a religious environment suggested that too much focus on Self contradicted the fabled virtues of humility. Loving others more than yourself was the recommended path.

As it turns out, I did indeed learn that, like other aspects of life, all begins within – including love. The spiritual journey itself is, in fact, about understanding and accepting the Self first, and then integrating with the outside world.

So then, the necessary question becomes, who or what IS the "Self"? Is it the body we see in the mirror? Is it the accomplishments that we complete each day? Is it the personality with which we greet the world? Is it the things we own or wear?

The Self is all these things. The Self also is the way in which we view the world, the way in which we make choices and decisions, the dreams and desires we have, our sense of humor, the way we operate.

Loving the Self begins with an absolutely necessary first step – LIKING the Self. There are certain things we tend to criticize ourselves for – not being thin enough, not being smart enough, not being good enough at one sport or another.

Much of my life I experienced a deep sense of self-consciousness around people, stemming from feeling like I wasn't good enough in some respects.

A few years ago, I was out taking a walk, and I suddenly saw an old, wizened man with a long, gray beard appear to me. I don't often have clairvoyant experiences, so this was unusual. The spirit brought up my self-image.

"Let's pretend for a moment that I am God and I created you." He said.

"Ummm ... OK ...." I replied hesitantly at the unusual concept coming from a guide. He actually did remind me of the archetypal patriarchal God.

"And, let's pretend that I created all that you see for you and I to enjoy together." He continued, ignoring my hesitancy. "Let's say that only you and I exist in this entire Universe, and I created it just for us, just for the two of us, so that we could experience it together."

"Uhhh.... Sure, yeah, OK." I shrugged, thinking that this unusual approach was really off-the-wall, and wondering where it would lead.

"Now, let's say that everyone you encounter as you live your life was also created to help you enjoy your life better; that everyone you meet has a role designed specifically to assist you in having a happier life. Everyone is here just for you." The spirit continued with an oblivious cheerfulness.

"Sure." I replied, waiting for the punch line.

He leaned forward in his chair, gazing at me through wizened eyes, a sly smile evident under his long white beard. "Would you still feel self-conscious?"

I went about three more paces before stopping dead in my tracks. The spirit sat back in his chair, chuckling, then vanished.

My head swam with the enormity of that thought. If I projected myself into a situation, such as the one just presented to me by this jovial spirit, a scenario where everyone was there simply to love me through this experience of this lifetime, that meant that what they may think of me simply becomes irrelevant, and .... Bingo, if I don't need to concern myself with what others think of me, and I am completely accepted – then the feelings of low self-worth and self-consciousness vanish into thin air! And THAT means – that I LIKE myself!

The way that I had learned to feel about myself in life was based upon the way that I believed others viewed me, the judgments I believed they held towards me. In that moment of erasing all those beliefs, stripping them all away, I was able in that moment of clarity to see only me – and I realized how much I like who I am!

It amazed me how profoundly that changed my attitude about life and others. Once I accepted myself, once I loved myself, loving and accepting others became automatic.

Once I reached that point of both liking and loving myself, my relationships with others quickly changed and became more loving as well. I released self-judgments and my experiences with others no longer mirrored those back to me. In a way, this pattern of love is really the Law of Attraction:

love for self comes from within; is expressed as love for others; and is reflected back through love from others.

What you put out into the Universe, what you create from within, from your being, from who you are – love – comes back in greater measure. When we do not restrict this flow with lower vibrational fears, expectations, or judgments, then this love is free to flow from within.

Love is ultimately the starting and the ending point of the human spiritual journey on Earth. We already ARE love when we come here. Then we experience situations which cause us to allow doubts, worries, and fears, which restrict the flow of love. Over a course of a myriad of lifetimes and countless experiences, we eventually return to a realization that the best answer to all situations is – love. And when we truly reach that realization, we are done having lifetimes on Earth.

Love is the beginning, and the ending, point of our journey here.

Passion

Your passions are your connection to All That Is.

We have already discussed happiness as a state of being, a natural one, how we are before we talk ourselves out of it. We have discussed joy as being a way in which we experience situations. Passion is the way in which we ENGAGE in situations in a joyful way.

Passion is an emotional experience. It is not a feeling. It combines desire and joy and sets them in motion. Passion is a choice, it is something we create and do. When we are expressing our passions we are very much in touch with the innermost core of our being.

When we are experiencing passion about something we are fully in the moment, and we are fully EXPERIENCING that moment. We are connecting who we are with what and how we are expressing who we are.

Passion is a highly magnetic choice in attracting more experiences to support our passions.

Grace

It is very intentional on my part to save this topic for the very last. You may, at some point, while contemplating how we create both enjoyable and un-enjoyable experiences for ourselves, and how things like thoughts and belief systems affect the process of creating, have found yourself wondering how we manage it all.

We can have such a tendency to allow one unpleasant experience, or one worry, or one fear, to so completely engulf us that we are not focused on any of the good that we do have in our lives. Sometimes we can push ourselves into such a state of mind that it seems we should be creating nothing but more and more difficult experiences for ourselves, experiences that confirm and solidify our worst fears, and that it can have a runaway effect. Then – suddenly – out of the blue something great happens to relieve our situation, and we can get back onto more solid emotional footing.

Fortunately for us, there is a loophole of sorts in the cosmic clockworks of the Universal Laws. If there weren't, we could eventually reach a point of despair in life from which we could attract only experiences which would push us further and further over the edge. That loophole is called grace.

Grace may come in many forms – unexpected assistance from a friend, a surprising and inexplicable change in a seemingly dire situation, something changing in just the nick of time.

Sometimes we call these coincidences, often they are accompanied by synchronicities, and some people call them miracles. However we choose to view them, they are provided through grace.

One of my guides, Mary, explained it in this way, using secular terminology:

God's Grace is provided in deserving cases where it is needed to:
1. *teach me to have faith*
2. *get me back to the right place*

3. *allow me an opportunity to apply and share and appreciate and honor God's Grace*
4. *give me an experience which can be taught to others.*

That's what God's Grace is for – the exceptions to the "Universal Law."

Patience is focusing on what is NOW, not what is not YET. Patience is focusing on HERE and NOW. For only in this one, present moment is God's Plan unfurled, God's Grace dispensed. Do you see this? It can be the ONLY focus, for nothing else IS.

Whenever you experience this within your own life – be sure to take a moment to express your appreciation to the Universe, then pass it on – by helping someone else, even a complete stranger, the next time an opportunity presents itself. Grace, when granted, is meant to be shared.

Beginning Anew

Each moment begins as we draw in our breath, and ends as we exhale. We have thousands upon thousands of them every day. Each and every one of those moments contains the potential for us to have an amazing experience, or an incredible life-changing realization. The potential in a single moment is truly, absolutely, and completely unlimited.

As each fresh moment arrives, what just occurred becomes forever the past, and a new future of our own making and choosing appears. We move from experience to experience, through emotion after emotion. At times we mechanically do the same routine things we do from day to day; at other times, we marvel at the surprises in life, and the simplest joys, and we wonder how it all works.

We tend to look outside ourselves to understand how, when and why life "happens" the way that it does. When we relate our own inner being to our experience of our environment – when we begin to make the connections between the inner world and the outer world, we begin to connect the dots and understand how life does work – and how great our own role is.

The process of conscious creation is a learning experience, an on-going one. But what we are learning really has nothing to do with the process of creating – and everything to do with learning to see who we really are. For we create and attract experiences that reflect aspects of who we are being.

As we grow along a spiritual path, we often develop the perception that we are "improving" because we are changing our thoughts, actions, and beliefs. But those are all things that are connected with the body, ego and personality we will discard at the end of this lifetime, as we have done so many times before. They are not who we really are.

Ultimately we do come to a realization that what we have been doing is peeling away the layers that don't "feel" like us, through experiences with other people in which we release aspects or actions that no longer resonate with us. And, ultimately, we realize what we have been doing all along –

becoming ever more in human form what we always were in the first place –
love.

Made in the USA
Charleston, SC
17 May 2010